OTHIL

Norse Ancestral Traditions

By
Bradley Murphey

Othil Norse Ancestral Traditions is published by Dark Moon Press
Ft. Wayne, Indiana

ISBN-13: 978-1532960376

For a full catalogue of Dark Moon's publications refer to
http://www.darkmoonpress.com

Or send an SASE to:
P.O. Box 11496, Ft. Wayne, Indiana, 46858-1496

Dedication

This book is dedicated to many people who have helped me put it together over the years. To Runestaven and all of its members, I thank you. To Red Rune Clan and its members, you were my first real inspiration. To Minnesota Heathens, who tolerated me, To Carthen, who, as my student, taught me. To Odin, who kicked my butt from time to time and kept me from going on tangents too entangled to get out of. To Kari Tauring, who gave me such good direction on Seidh work and working with drop spindles. Finally, to Charles Barnard, who helped me edit this book. He did his best to persuade me that English is NOT my first language.

But this book is especially dedicated to Teresa. You are my friend, my teacher, my lover, my partner and so much more. The one to whom I could turn at any time. Your encouragement and insight has been invaluable. To me you are more precious than gold.

Table of Contents

Forward 1

Synthesis 4

What is Mythology 7

Norse Mythology 9

The Deities 11

    Odin 12

    Tyr 12

    Loki 12

    Frigg 13

    Njord 13

    Freyja 14

    Frey/ Ing 15

    Thor 15

    Heimdall 16

    Vili and Ve 17

    Baldur 17

    Hod 17

    Idun 17

    Braggi 18

    Skadhi 18

    Sif 18

    Ull 18

    Var 19

    Sunna and Mani 19

    Od 19

    Gefjun 20

Other Beings 21

    Jotn 21

    Mimir 22

    Norns 23

    Surt 23

    Liekin 23

    Fenrir 23

    Jormungand 24

    Nydhogg 24

Gullveig/Heid..24
Hrymthurs 25
Thrym...25
Thiazzi..25
Angrboda and Aurboda................................26
Elves and Dwarves..27
Elven Races...28
Dwarves 29
Other Legendary Beings and ARtifacts 31
Einharjar..31
Valkyrjes 31
Berserkers 31
Asmegir...32
Sleipnir...32
Brisingamen 32
Mjollnir 33
Hamingja..33
Myrk-Riders 33
Norse View of Creation 35
Ymir and the Underworld..............................35
Creation of Midgard....................................37
Six Elements of Man....................................37
The Beginning (and end) of the World.....................41
The First War 42
Ragnarok 43
Government and Society...................................45
Migrations 49
Group Relationships......................................55
Celebrations 59
BlÓts and sumbls 63
Blóts...63
Rite of the Sonar Golt 63
The Order of Horns......................................64
Sumbl..64
Major BlÓts Throughout the Year.........................65
Midsvaetrablót   January 12th - 14th...................67

Odinirveidhifor   February 6 67
Heimdalsdag   March 15........................ 68
Sigurdblót/Somrdag   April 22 68
Baldursdag   May 2 68
Midsomerblót   June 15........................ 68
Freyjasdag   August 15 69
Leif Ericksonsdag   October 9...... 70
Vinternal/Vaetrablót/Disablót   October 14 70
Calendars, Times and Seasons.................................. 73
    Harvest Month 73
    Days of the Week... 74
Sacred Weapons.. 77
What is Ritual?... 81
Norse Ritual 83
Galdr and Seidh.. 87
Runes... 91
    The Elder Futhark 94
    Organizing The Runes 96
    Meanings Of The Runes 97
Fe/ Fehu 98
Ur/Uruz 99
Thurs/Thurisaz 100
Os/Ansuz... 101
Radh/Raidho 102
Kaun/Kenaz.. 103
Gyf/Gebo... 104
Wyn/Wunjo.. 105
Hagl/Hagalaz.. 106
Nauth/Nauthiz 107
Is/Isa.. 108
Ar/Jera.. 109
Eoh/Eiwaz... 110
Pertho/Peord.. 111
Eolh/Algiz... 112
Sigl/Sowelo.. 113
Tyr/Tiwaz... 114

Bjarkan/Berkano 115
Eh/Ehwaz 116
Madr/Mannaz 117
Logr/Laguz.. 118
Ing/Inguz 119
Daeg/Dagaz 120
Othil/Othila 121
Rune Casting.. 123
   Single Rune Spread............................... 124
   Three Rune Spread................................ 124
   Celtic Cross 125
   Rune Cast 125
Rune Magic 127
   Rista 128
   Radha 128
   Fa.. 128
   Feista 129
   Bidja 129
   Blota 129
   Senda 130
   Soa.. 130
Birthrunes.. 133
Rune Stones in America............................. 135
Vikings In America 143
Herbs – ABC's 145
   How Herbs May Be Used 145
   The List of Herbs 146
Trees and Woods....................................... 150
   Yew 150
   Oak 150
   Birch.. 150
   Cedar 150
   Pine 151
   Ash 151
   Elm 151
   Apple... 151

Hazel 151
A Little About Metals 153
    Iron 153
    Brass 153
    Silver 153
    Gold 153
    Copper and Tin (also see Brass) 154
Poetic and Musical Styles 155
Prayers and Songs 159
    Brunhilde's Prayer 159
    Prayer to Activate a Spoken Rune Spell 159
    Prayer over the Sonar-Golt 159
    Consecration of the Horn 160
    Prayer for the Spring Planting 160
    Old Norse Hammer Hallowing 160
    Delling's Morning Prayer 161
    Ridha Vit (a prayer for the dead) 161
Glossary 163
Pronunciation Guide 167
Additional Notes 169
    Hod 169
    Leikn 169
    The Asmegir 169
    Calendars and Blóts and Celebrations 169
    Odinirveidhifor 170
    Three Cups 170
    Radh 170
    Hymiskvidha 171
Bibliography 173
Recommended Readings 175
    Also Recommended 175

FORWARD

Othil is a book about Norse tradition. There are many such books being published today, but, what makes this book different, is that the processes contained herein, work. Through many years of research and experimentation, I have discovered basic principles that focus magical and ritual intents, which are based on a foundation of ancient (and not so ancient) cultural understandings. This book has, therefore, gone through many transformations.

Keep in mind that this book is not meant to be contradictory to someone else's book (except in spots). Some of those seeming contradictions come from the study of the peoples in different regions. Some are from the study of different eras. All of these viewpoints are valid, just different. So this book is not meant as a response to misinformation (except in spots). There are so many belief systems, which fall under the heading of Norse/Teutonic that to say one work is definitive and another is not, limits one's own experience and study. Some of what I have found will seem controversial. I will do my best to explain myself, either by laying out the logic, or by giving references in the ancient literature.

You'll find the section on Runes to be much different than what you may have read in other books. Much of this difference is because the Runes are dialectic. I find it impossible to believe that the Runes did not change meaning over such a vast area as Europe, or that they did not change over such a broad expanse of time. To suggest so is to take the reader for granted. Look at the changes our own language has gone through in the last 200 years, alone. Words have different meanings or emphases from subculture to subculture. There has been a move by many authors to standardize the meaning and pronunciations of the runes, disregarding all others. This is not a bad goal, in and of itself, but it places limits on the Runes. You will find that many Runes have more than one meaning.

You will also find certain relationships between the deities are treated differently than what you may have read so far. So many books today, accept a viewpoint of these relationships that is not, necessarily a Norse view and certainly not an East Norse view. In many cases, though they came from the same cultural foundation, the understandings evolved differently.

I must interject here; I will be using the word 'Norse' to designate those tribes/peoples/cultures, which we see as Scandianvian, while I use the words 'Germanic' and 'Teutonic' more in reference to those peoples associated with the mainland of Europe. Belive me, it's easier in Swedish, which uses words like 'Deutch' for the contemporary people of Germany, while using the word 'Germanic' to designate the ancient peoples.

In speaking of the deities, you'll find that many have more than one name. There may be many reasons behind this, but I narrow it down to three. The first is the skaldic tradition of assimilation. When an ancient tribe was conquered or somehow assimilated into a greater tribe, they did not as much 'do away' with the old gods. Instead, they learned all they could about those gods and gave their own gods new names to be known by (ex. Veur or Hlorithi becomes Thor, Hlin becomes Frigg, etc).

Another reason for this myriad of names is the use of epithets. These were not, originally, names, as such, but, rather handles describing their character, lifestyle or some great deed (ex. Sithgrani or Gagnrath for Odin, Mengladh for Freyja. For that matter, 'Frey' and 'Freyja' may fit into this category). These types of names may better fit the description of a kenning than a name, per se.

Still another reason may have to do with the skalds again. Many sagas and songs were written about events or personages, whose characters scream the reference of a deity, hero, or well-known event. Examples of this can range from Fjolvismal (Svipdag and Mengladh) to Shakespear's Hamlet or King Lear (no, I'm not suggesting that Shakespear was a skald. I am citing examples of that style).

I did not use any diacritical markings in this book; primarily, because most English speaking people aren't familiar with them. Most diacritical symbols did not come into use until the early 1800's, anyway. There is a pronunciation guide at the back of the book, which will be helpful to those who desire to wish to know more about how Old Norse words should sound.

Wherever possible, I have either cited references to connect the names or laid out the resoning behind those connections. Throughout the book, you will find references to verses in Eddic

2

tales and Sagas. Unless otherwise noted, the referenced verses are taken from the Hollander version of the Poetic Edda.

I wish you well. I wish you success.
Was du Heil!
Bradley Murphey
2016

SYNTHESIS

Synthesis is a word that a lot of people are afraid of and needn't be. When something is synthetic, it does not mean it is not real. It means that two or more things have been put together to form a new thing. What any Pagan does, what any Pagan group does, is a synthesis of old ways and new ideas and mindsets.

When we talk about following ancient ways, synthesis is a concept that is vitally important to be honest about. There is relatively little that has been handed down to us from the ancients about the ritual processes they followed. This is true in most traditions. I won't say all. I don't know them all. And neither does anyone else.

Nevertheless, there are clues and bits we can glean that give us insight to how ritual was performed. These come from studying Cultural Anthropology and Archeology as much as historical documents. For instance: was the ancient culture prone to ritual (some were more than others)? Again, what was their belief about the cosmos and creation? Were deities invited to be present at ritual and religious services? I could go on, but you get the idea.

Not one group that I am aware of practices ritual exactly the same way they did in the ancient times. This is also because of the evolution of culture. People change and cultures change when new ideas are introduced and become part of the culture itself.

I met a group, once, who told me that they were strictly Norse. They told me they followed the old ways and disregarded anything else. Upon further discussion, this group told me that they only use Sandalwood incense in their rituals. What they didn't understand was that Sandalwood comes from India, the Middle East and Asia. The ancient Vikings would not have used it until later in history. They would have used something from the world they knew around them.

Now, I have nothing against Sandalwood. I find it a very effective incense and use it myself on occasion. But it has been synthesized into pagan culture. Unless you're doing ritual to Kali or Shiva, it was not part of the ancient practice. I am exaggerating a bit with that statement, but I do it to prove a point. The point is that the physical trappings of ritual and magic come from the world surrounding the culture. An imported trapping can be added to an existing ritual process but this is also a form of synthesis, however ancient.

There is not one writer on Norse traditions who expounds solely on ancient practices. What they outline is a synthesis of their studies and the accepted practices and understandings of their readership. This is not a bad thing, necessarily, but it must be understood. What I do is also a synthesis, but it is based on cultural understandings of ancient Norse ritual practices, not on Wiccan Circle construction.

The Wiccan Circle format lends itself very well to working with many different deities from many different cultures and becomes a good foundation for many forms of worship. Don't throw it out simply because it didn't come from the particular culture you are studying. Wicca, in and of itself, is a synthesis, but a good one and an effective one for many people.

The word 'Wicca' has is roots in the Old Saxon word 'wicce' (pronounced vee-cha). The word 'witch' is a derivative of that same word. But the Saxons had the same cultural roots as the Norse and may have even been a splinter group of the Sviar who settled in what is now Sweden long before the newer Norse tribes migrated to that part of the world.

The word 'wicce' came down to the Saxons from the Old Norse word 'vitki'. These were what we would call today, solitary practitioners; magic users and power workers. Consequently, ancient "Wiccans" would have really been of Norse distinction (don't get upset with me over that; take it up with your ancestors).

Because of certain cultural understandings of the time (roughly 2 - 4000 years ago) I seriously doubt that certain things that are done today in the name of Wicca were practiced back then. For instance, in come eras, a man having the top of his shirt open in public was considered naked and this was an offense punishable by stoning or hanging. Yes, the ancient laws forbade such public displays and the punishment was clearly outlined. Also, many temples to the Norse gods did not allow weapons of any kind within their walls. How are these two examples reconciled with contemporary practices like Sky-clad (being unclothed in ritual) and the use of Athames (a ritually used knife)? These practices have been assimilated into Pagandom as acceptable. This is an example of synthesis.

The ancient Norse accepted only three natural, creative elements – at least in the way that we see them. Air and Fire were not seen as elements. Their cultural philosophy only supported three elements; Ice-cold Seawater, The Power of Earth, and Creative Wisdom. This leads to all sorts of interesting translations between their culture and ours. The only way to satisfy it is to synthesize their belief structure into our own cultural understanding.

We can also see how traditions changed in times gone by. How our grandparents celebrated certain holidays is not, necessarily, how we celebrate them, today. More to the point, how our grandparents celebrated certain holidays is not, necessarily, how their ancestors celebrated the same holidays. We learn from our ancestors, but we teach synthesis to our children. So, synthesis is not a bad thing, but it must be accepted honestly. When we do so, we are much more able to place the power of ritual where it needs to be.

WHAT IS MYTHOLOGY

The term mythology is used in any number of ways. I've heard it used derogatorily, accusing someone of making a false statement. People also use it to differentiate from history. The idea is that history is factual and evidential while mythology has no basis in reality. Even though the word is used this way, this statement is not completely true.

There is an old saying: "History is written by the victor." This means that whoever is in power has the right to call his/her own opinion factual. History books are re-written time and time again to 'conclusively prove' the previously held view as slanted, biased or an outright lie set forth to keep the previous regime in the best possible light. A good example of this is how the Weimar Government was portrayed while Hindenburg was President of Germany, as opposed to how it was presented under the succeeding Nazi regime. 'New evidence' is always being revealed to disprove what historians 'thought they knew.' History, then, is as changeable as personal opinion.

Mythology, on the other hand, is much less changeable. It may evolve over time and more may be added to it. But rarely does it change completely without becoming a new mythology. We can see this in Norse mythology in the stories about Loki. What his role was originally is not what he became, over time. It takes a long time to get from Fire God to Trickster. But he was still Loki.

The word 'mythology' is based on the Greek word, 'muthos,' which means a story or tale having to do with deities, heroes and archetypal images. Nowhere in the basic definition does it imply that a myth is untrue. That idea comes from other contextual uses of the word. This use is what the word has evolved into.

On this foundation, we can understand that any (or, at least most) religion is based in mythology. This gives most religions, if not all, something in common. If we could look for commonalities between religions we could promote understanding and foster mutual respect. That which we fear, we seek to destroy. Chief Dan George is quoted as saying;

If you talk to the animals, they will talk to you and you will get to know each other. If you do not talk to them, you will not know them and what you do not know, you fear. What one fears, one destroys.

Mythology gives us a foundation in understanding a culture, its world view, its understanding of creation, power, ethics and morals. Mythology also gives us a body of lore by which we comprehend deity and its place in our lives. Mythology gives us goals to aspire to.

In most mythology that I have read, one can find historical points of reference. This may be the name of a king, a historic voyage, a migration, war, possibly a great discovery. The possibilities are endless. Most mythology was handed down as part of the oral tradition of a people long before the written word. It was important to connect the ideas as true events in the listener's mind and to suggest a historical point of reference gave the storyteller that edge. Using a familiar reference helped to make the story come alive for the listener. But in tracing the history of the same event we may not find the same chronology.

A prime example is that in the Middle Ages and later, it was generally accepted that Moses, in the Judeo-Christian mythology, led a whole nation of people out of slavery, across a desert and to a new land that they could call their own. It was also accepted that these slaves built the pyramids and the really cool sites in Egypt and – as slaves- farmed the best land Egypt had to offer during the time of Ramses. But Archeology has proven that this people never existed as a nation in slavery, nor, have they found any traces of the culture in the farming area known as Goshen.

But the proof that everybody turned to that it happened was the mythological writings. Does this make the lessons in those writings invalid? No. The historical points of reference in those writings were added to make the lessons come alive for the listener. So what is the real history of this nation? Well, someday we might discover it. History changes. But a people's mythology rarely does.

Mythology is not untrue. Mythology may even allude to historical events. But mythology gives us something great to aspire to that is based in the culture of a people.

8

NORSE MYTHOLOGY

Norse mythology is an evolution of many ancient mythologies. It is an amalgamation or synthesis, if you will. Some of the elements can be traced back to Ancient Persia at least 3-4000 years ago. There is even evidence that Classical Greek and what became Norse/ Germanic mythologies may have had some common roots. What we commonly refer to as Norse Mythology is really Proto-Norse/Germanic and is hard to separate due to the early migrations of the peoples in the Baltic Region as they traveled in all directions. The major portion of this migratory period started roughly in the 300's BCE. From approximately 800 CE to 1100 CE is the period we refer to as the Viking Era. However, it is difficult to separate the later migrational and expansion eras from the Viking Age. I, therefore, refer to the Viking Age as starting around 300 CE and finishing up in the early 1100's.

The Nordic/Germanic tribes seemed to have the philosophy that conquering another tribe did not mean doing away with the religious beliefs of the vanquished peoples. Instead, the Skalds – singers and poets who acted as lore keepers and historians -- assimilated those gods into the greater whole of the lore. The conquering tribe would adopt some traditions while the conquered tribe would adopt others. Ultimately, this practice helped to make them all one people. Because of this assimilation and expansion, we have a number of deities who were worshipped over a large part of Europe, though they may have been viewed differently from place to place.

Here are a couple of examples: In Scandinavia Tyr is known as the god of Justice. He is the warrior's god with one hand (due to placing it in Fenrir's mouth). Odin is his father and we have no reference to his mother's name. Odin is the chief of all the Aesir and is also father to others, such as Baldur and Hod. But in some parts of Mainland Europe, Tyr is the chief god and is the lawgiver. They had no early reference to his having only one hand. In the south, Donnar (commonly seen as the equivalent of Thor) is the thunder god, and is the protector of the common man. In the north, Thor is the protector of the gods, as well as the common man.

Just as in Greek tradition, where the gods were descended from the Titans, the Norse gods were descended from another race of beings; the Jotn (commonly translated as Giants). Ymir was the first, and from him are descended Bor and Bestla, who bore three sons: Odin, Hoenir and Lodur (also known as Vili and Ve). These three killed their grandfather, Ymir, and created the worlds and all beings from his body, bones and blood. Man and woman were created from two trees; Ash and Elm, respectively.

Incidentally, the Norse creation story gives us a good indication about how magic was viewed. All things already exist, but can be modified or altered to make a new thing. This saves us the trouble of making something from scratch. Use what you've got to your advantage. This is also true of the Runes. Odin did not create the Runes. The Havamal says he "caught them up, wailing." He took them to himself and mastered their power and wisdom. In so doing, they became his and he is therefore known as the Father of the Runes. But they were created by the Norns; Urd, Verthandi and Skuld (see Voluspasaga 20).

THE DEITIES

It is interesting to note that only one parent needs to be deity for the child to be considered deity. The other parent could be Human, Elvin or Jotn, though, Jotn happened most frequently. It is also important to add, here, that all the races came originally from Jotn stock.

One might also keep in mind that the term Jotn may have been used to denote an older race of deities who had fallen out of favor, as well as the terrible creatures that we think of when we think of the giants. In that respect, they could be likened to the Titans of Greek Mythology. In other words, the Jotn may well have been branded with a more derogatory name, that of Thurs. It is also possible that the term Thurs took on more derogatory meaning over time and use – quite like the words Pagan and Heathen.

The Norse deities are not Germanic counterparts to the Roman or Greek deities. Making such a correlation was a practice promoted by Tacitus, Julius Caesar and other writers of the ancient world simply to give their readers a perspective based on their own foundational beliefs. Keep in mind that the Romans saw themselves as a sort of 'master race' and therefore, whatever was learned from other cultures was filtered through that understanding.

There are many branches of the Norse deities but they all seem to filter down to the Aesir, the Vanir and the Jotn. Though Odin was the father of many of them, he was not the father of all the gods counted among the Aesir. He is called Alfather because he is the supreme god; not because he spawned all other deities.

Nor, was Frigg the mother of all the gods, though she has children of both Aesiric and Vanic descent.

Below is a SHORT list of some of the more principle deities in the Norse/Germanic traditions. This is not a full list, but it will get you started. Please note that some of the associations are different than what you may have studied in the past. The descriptions are taken from recorded mythology, not assumed tradition. Also, the East Norse perspective answers some of the questions about the genealogies of the Aesir and the Vanir.

11

ODIN

Also known as Alfather, Odin has numerous names. He is the chief god of the Aesir and the god of Wisdom, War and Poetry. Odin is a shape shifter and frequently travels the worlds in disguise. From him we have been given the Runes and Galdrwerk. Odin has two ravens, Hugin and Munin, who traverse the Earth, bringing all knowledge to him. He also travels frequently, with two wolves, Frekki and Geri. His symbol of office is his spear, named Gungnir.

TYR

There are two very separate and distinct gods by this name. The first is Tyr, the chief god in parts of Mainland Europe, especially in the South. His attributes are justice, peace and a good-hearted nature. He was worshipped above Odin (Wodan) partly because he was more approachable. They saw Wodan as aloof to humans, except, possibly, royalty and nobility. This Tyr is not Odin's son. Instead his lineage is entirely Jotn: Hymir being his father and his grandmother (or mother, depending on the translation) is a nine-headed, very ugly and hateful Jotn. This Tyr did not lose his hand to Fenrir and was not worshipped as 'the One-Handed God.' This is the Tyr that is personified in Hymiskvida.

The second Tyr is worshipped in the north and Scandinavia. He is a god of justice and, in some cases, justice through selfless sacrifice (ex; losing his hand to Fenrir). This Tyr is the son of Odin and some sources say Frigg, while others list his mother as Sif (personally, I subscribe to the tradition that his mother is Frigg). He is not a war god, but a warrior's god. He protects warriors whose cause is just (*Sigrdrifumal 7*).

The confusion comes because, in the south and the north, both gods were considered Aesiric and both assume authority over Justice.

LOKI

Malevolent and scheming, Loki later became known as the god of mischief and a trickster. He is a shape shifter who has sired and born children in other forms. He is not of the Aesir at all, but wholly of Jotn descent and there is evidence that he existed as a fire god in a pantheon older than the Aesir. He is the father of Jormungand (the Midgard Serpent), Liekin (the dis of Disease), Fenrir (the great Wolf) and many monster children, including the Trolls. But he is also the *mother* of Sliepnir, Odin's eight-legged horse. At Ragnarok, he fights against the gods and seeks to destroy them. He and Heimdall kill each other there.

It is interesting to note that, because of the blood-pact between Loki and Odin, the Aesir cannot kill him. At the conclusion of Lokasenna, he is chased down and chained, but he is not killed, though, that's what everybody wanted.

FRIGG

The wife of Odin, she is actually of Vanic descent and is the sister of Njord. Frigg is the goddess of Wisdom, Motherhood and the Earth as well as the Passage of Death, though this should not be confused with the authority over death held by Hel. As all Vanir, she had the gift of foresight.

Frigg has a confusing lineage. Where some sources list her as the mother of Thor, other sources call her the daughter of Fjorgyn – making her at least his half sister. The name Fjorgyn for Frigg is actually the feminized form of Fjorgynr, who was her father.

She is also known as Jord (Erde..Earth). What we do know is that Frigg is the mother of Frey and Freyja and she is not Freyja. That problem is because the term freyja (meaning, 'lady') was also used in ancient times to refer to both of them.

NJORD

The Sea god, he is also the god of acquired wealth. His animal associations include the Swan (which is sacred to him). He is adorned with the Eagle and the Heron. His first wife was his sister, Frigg, with which he fathered Freyja and Frey (*Ynglingasaga ch 4*). His second wife was Skadhi. Njord is Vanic and, along with his twin children, offered himself as hostage to the Aesir after the war which nearly destroyed both godly races. He is not mentioned as ever holding a leadership position among the Vanir, but that is assumed because of his presiding over the Sea and prosperity, which is as important to the Vanir as war is to the Aesir. It is also assumed so because he led the Vanir in the war with the Aesir, where he broke the gates of Asgard with his battle axe.

Some of the oldest altars in Scandinavia were to Njord. After Ragnarok, his time of hostage is over and he goes back to Vanaheim (*Vafthrudismal 38-39*). However, there is an old Swedish tradition involving a feast to honor Njord because of his

13

death, since, during his lifetime, there had been peace and prosperity. I could find little verifiable information on this Sumbl, and therefore left it out of the calendar of feasts.

FREYJA

The twin sister of Frey, she is the goddess of love, fertility, beauty, and desire. There is also a darker side to Freyja, as she is also the goddess who brought Seidh magic to the Aesir (*Ynglingasage ch 4*). Like her brother, Frey, she has authorities over wealth and prosperity. She is the daughter of Njord and Frigg and therefore wholly of the Van Race. The name Freyja means Lady (as in Lord and Lady) and is actually her title, not her name. Like most of the gods, she has many names, but her best known ones are Mardoll and Menglad. Freyja also presides over the sacrifices to the gods (*Ynlingasaga ch 4 and ch. 13*).

She is the most beautiful of all the goddesses. But she is married to Od (*Ynglindasaga ch. 13*), whom she loves and seeks desperately. In her search for her lost husband, she wept tears of gold upon the Earth. Where her tears fell into the sea, they became amber. She has two daughters, Hnoss (Ornament) and Gersemi (She who Becomes). The cat and the Boar are sacred to her.

According to Fjolsvinnsmal, Freyja, who is given the name Mengladh in the lay, has nine maidens who attend her and act on her will. They are:

THJOTHVARA	Leader of the nine
EIR	Dis of healing
HLIF	Shield
HLEIFTHRASA	Obstinate Shield
AURBODA	Freyja's sword-carrier
BRIDH	Friendly
FRIDH	Handsome
BLEIK	Fair one
BJORT	Bright (shining) one

In all cases, we know the attributes of each by virtue of the names or from other texts, in which they appear. They are not the Valkyrjes, as some have suggested. The Nine Attendants as Shield Maidens of Freyja is a later addition to the mythology; most likely due to the additions of Death and War to Freyja's offices. It is my

14

opinion that this list was first devised by a Skald, who did not know the "Mytho-History" well enough.

First of all, Hlif and Hleifthrasa are the Asmegir (please read that section). Leifthrasa is a masculine name (-sa meaning 'HE who' * Note: the names are spelled both ways in different texts, but the words have very different meanings). As such, he never would have been a shield maiden. That being said, the qualities, or duties, they have been given in this list have nothing to do with their names or their descriptions in other texts. Second of all is the inclusion of Eir as a goddess of healing. In a later invention in the Southern Germanies, Eir was made the sister of Tyr. The problem is that the Old Norse word, 'eir' means Bronze or Copper and has nothing to do with physical healing.

Aurboda, as 'Sword-Bearer 'for Freyja cannot be verified in the early texts. Aurboda is identical with Angrboda (*see section on Other Beings*). As Angrboda, she is the mother of Loki's 'monster children,' including Fenrir and the Trolls. But as Aurboda, she is also the mother of Frey's love, Gerde. Angrboda is a sworn enemy of the Aesir and the Vanir, but, as Aurboda, she taught the "Dark Arts," to Freyja, who then turned around and taught Seidh to the Aesir.

As I mentioned earlier,Fjolvinnsmal calls Freyja by the name Mengladh, meaning 'Glad in her necklace,' thus, alluding to the Brisingamen. But, vss 7-8 also allude to her authorities in prosperity and wealth.

FREY/ ING
The twin of Freyja and the son of Njord and Frigg. Frey is the god of the Earth, taking after his mother, but he is responsible for distributing the riches of his father. Even though wealth comes *from* Njord, it comes *through* Frey. Life and fertility are his domains. His animals are the Boar and the Stag. Like his sister, his name is the title meaning Lord. Frey is of the Vanic race of gods, but is also known as "the best of the Aesir". Frey is god of the Elves, having received Alfheim as a tooth-fee gift after his birth.

THOR
The son of Odin and Frigg, he is the strongest of the gods and is the protector of Asgard. Known for his thunderous attitude, he has

15

a belt which increases his strength ten-fold, and has his war hammer, Mjollnir.

A slightly later development in his myology made Thor the protector of the common man. This is a logical extension, since we are the creation of the gods. He, therefore, is protecting the gods' interests. Thor spends much time battling the Jotn and Hrymthurs (Frost giants). He is married to Sif, who bore him two sons; Magni and Modi and a daughter, Gefjun. Magni and Modi are deities who survive Ragnarok and take us into the future with Baldur.

There is conjecture as to what Thor's lineage is. There are ancient texts, which refer to him as the son of Frigg. Other texts, such as Harbarzljod, call him the son of Fjorgyn, as also the mother of Frigg. Either way, we do know that he is Vanic (*Hymiskvida 3*). In this verse, Aegir vows vengeance on the Vanir because of Thor's forcing him to make mead. Why the Vanir and not the Aesir? Because his lineage was carried through the mother's line. Thor's being Vanic accounts for Gefjun's gift of foresight, as it would have been passed down to her.

HEIMDALL
Heimdall is also of Vanic descent, as he was born in the Underworld to nine mothers – the maidens who turn The World-Mill. This brings up something I should mention here: Not all Vanic gods were from Vanaheim. Heimdall is the watcher of the gods and guards Bifrost Bridge from intruders who may want to enter Asgard. Heimdall is armed with both sword and hunting horn, the Gjallarhorn, which he blows when help is needed at the bridge. It is said that his hearing is so acute that he can hear grass growing and that his eyesight is so acute that he can see 100 leagues away. He also has foresight (*Thrymskvida 15*) and can see the future, which is one of the gifts associated with the Vanir.

The worship of Heimdall is older than that of the Aesir. He is also known as Rig. Rig progenerated the classes of man, thus, giving structure to man's culture. The name Rig has very ancient Indo-European roots, the word meaning 'praise verse' in Sanskrit. Whether this is an actual connection to Heimdall, has been postulated for a long time. If this is so, Rig would not have been his name but became such in the same way we use the names Frey and Freyja.

16

VILI AND VE

The brothers of Odin, Lodur and Hoenir are also known by their titles, Vili (will) and Ve (banner). Together, the three of them are responsible for the death of Ymir and the creation of the world and all things, therein. After the creation of Midgard and the separation made between Asgard, Midgard and the Underworld, Hoenir (Ve) and Lodur (Vili) became the chiefs of the Vanir. We hear very little of them after this.

It is Hoenir who is sent to the Vanir as hostage, along with Mimir. When the Vanir did not trust Hoenir's counsel, they killed Mimir, suspecting duplicity.

BALDUR

Known as the Shining One, Baldur is the son of Odin and Frigg. He was the most beautiful and best loved of all the gods, until an arrow, shot by his brother, Hodr, killed him. He now resides in Helheim and will not be released till Ragnarok. Baldur is a god of peace and is one of many who can resolve conflicts. As the Shining One, archelogically, he has been seen as the sun god. Baldur brings the hope of a brighter future. Early writings indicate that he, like his brother Hodr, was a great warior.

HOD

Also called Hodr, he is the twin brother of Baldur and is his antithesis. Where Baldur is a god of peace, Hod is a god of war. Contrary to popular belief, he is not blind. Only Snorri called him the blind god. (*See Additional Notes*) In the old tales, he was subverted by Loki to kill Baldur and, as such, was 'blinded' by Loki's lies. Enough of the old stories have survived to show that he had a keen eye, when it came to weaponry. Before Baldur's death, Hod was also his brother's protector.

IDUN

Worship of Idun as a vegetation goddess is much older than the worship of the Aesir, and may go back as far as the original inhabitants of Scandinavia, the Gaets. She is, therefore, a prime example of the skaldic tradition of deification through marriage (*Lokasenna*). She is the daughter of Ivalde and an unnamed Sundis and that makes her Alfr (Elvish) by birth. It also makes her the half-sister of Egil and Voland.

17

Her importance in Asgard is well known. She was in charge of the Apples of Youth and distributes them among the Aesir and Vanir. With these, she keeps the gods young and strong.

BRAGGI

The Aesiric god of Skaldic poetry and song. As such, he would take direction from Odin, himself in this matter. This also makes him responsible for history and the keeping of oral tradition. The Braggarkupp (*see the Order of Horns*) is named for him and that means that he has authority to bless the oaths that men make.

SKADHI

Although she is wholly Jotn by descent, she is counted among the gods. Skadhi married twice– Njord and Ull. As Jotn, she is from an older race of gods that included Ran, Aegir, Loki, Thjassi (her father) and Thrym. As such, Skadhi rounds out the pantheon, which also includes the Sea, Death, Fire, and Weather.

Skadhi is the goddess of Winter. Her beauty is as the beauty of ice or the glisten of snow in sunlight. Skadhi is the goddess of the Winter Hunt and the matron goddess of skiing and skating. She is also a warrior, who was willing to go up against all of Asgard to seek vengeance for the death of Thiassi.

SIF

We know Sif best as the wife of Thor, but we hear little about her before that point. She is an elder goddess of grain and harvest. When grain ripens in the field, it turns golden. Such is Sif's hair. She has a shy, but willing attitude, as a fertility goddess, and it is in her nature to placate those around her in an effort to make peace (*Lokasenna 53*). In an earlier saga, Loki cut off her hair, but the dwarves replaced it, as a gift, with gold. Prior to her marriage to Thor and becoming an Asa-goddess, she was married to Egil, brother of Volund.

ULL

A rather misunderstood god, though he needn't be. Ull is the male counterpart to Skadhi. He is the god of skiing and the hunt. Skating and skiing were not invented by him, but rather, by his father Egil (also called Orvandel in the Younger Edda and by Saxo Gramaticus) who also invented Archery. Ull mastered these skills

18

and was more adept at them than his father. Ull then became the god associated with them.

Ull is the son of Sif and an unnamed father. Orvandel/Egil was her second husband and Ull's stepfather. Thor became her third husband. Before the First War, Ull followed his mother to Asgard and was known by the Aesir as one of the great archers. Along with the skills named above, Ull was also known for his wisdom and leadership. During the Age of Discontent, when the Aesir and the Vanir were at war, Ull was placed in the High Seat while Odin was banished from Asgard. Upon Odin's return, they made peace and Ull was allowed to stay. We hear very little about him since that time.

VAR

Var is the goddess who enforces contracts and commitments. It is she who hears our oaths to make sure we keep them. This is especially true when it comes to making oaths of love and marriage (*Thrymskvida 30*) but she hears any oaths made before gods and other authorities. She is part of Frigg's retinue. Though Var seems to have a minor role in the mythology, she has important, day-to-day duties.

SUNNA AND MANI

Sunna and Mani were the children of Mundilferi, who also enslaved them. Odin took pity on the two children and rescued them from their father. They were, then, fostered by Tyr before being given the duties they perform now. At Ragnarok, two wolves swallow up the Sun and Moon.

Technically, they are not deities, but have been deified through their offices. Sunna drives the wagon of the Sun and her brother Mani drives the wagon of the moon. In other words, under strict Norse tradition, the Sun is Female and the Moon is Male. These beings are different than Day and Night (Dag and Nott), where the genders are reversed. The gender balance then is that where Day is masculine, the Sun is feminine. Where Night is feminine, the Moon is masculine.

OD

Od is the erstwhile husband of Freyja. While she is seeking him, Od is on quest to find her. Od is a warrior of considerable prowess and heart. But he is also a lover and peacemaker. During the Age of Discontent, Od sided with the Vanir and participated in the storming of Asgard.

Od is more widely known by another name, Svipdag (see Fjolsvinnsmal 41-42 and compare Ynglingasaga ch 13). His mother, Groa, gave him the use of magical song when he went on his journey to find his love, Freyja. According to most accounts, his father is Egil.

GEFJUN

There is very little in the commonly accepted Edda about her. She is the daughter of Thor and Sif. Through Thor, she inherited the gift of foresight, which makes her Vanic. Even Odin marveled at her accuracy (*Lokasenna 21*). As the daughter of Sif, she has inherited authorities in the area of prosperity. Even her name is a derivative of the Old Norse word, *gefa*, meaning gift. It's important to note, here that Gefjun is a different name than Gefn, which is one of the many names of Freyja. The confusion is that both names are derived from *gefa*.

Lokasenna 20 makes reference to how desirable she is and how willing she is to make love. I have also seen her described as a goddess of dance and music. I find no references corroborate this. Though she is not specifically named in Alvismal, it is my opinion that she is the object of the Dwarf Alvis' affection.

Gefjun is responsible for separating the island of Zealand in Denmark from Sweden and dragging it there by way of her four sons, whom she turned into oxen (*see Ynglingasaga*). She also married Skjold and the two of them became the progenitors of the Danish royal line.

Worship of Gefjun includes the giving of gifts and sexual intimacy.

20

OTHER BEINGS

It is difficult to separate other races of beings from the Aesir and the Vanir. Partly, because many of them were worshipped as deities before the new religion – meaning, Aesir worship -- came to the Northern regions. And it is partly due to the fact that the Aesir and Vanir are descended from some of them.

It is important to know about them, however. They are not, necessarily, unfriendly to the gods.

JOTN

The Jotn were the original beings to inhabit Midgard and the Underworld. The terms Etin, Jotn and Thurs are not classifications of these beings. Etin is Anglicized from Jotn and it is therefore same word. Thurs is a term that was used derogatorily to refer to them. It is a word that the early skalds would have used to cast a dim light on the old gods (the Jotn).

The beings we call Giants, or Jotn, were the elder gods from whom the Aesir and the Vanir are descended. Some of the Aesir have counterparts among the Jotn, which is not antithetical as much as they were part of the cultural evolution. For PR purposes, the godhi and the skalds referred to them in negative terms – such as Thurs. At the same time, they had to account for the existence of the gods.

The mythology has the groups intermarry and have children, thereby giving its stamp of approval on worshipping these deities. Some became good guys, like Loki (well, sort of). In his original form, he was a god of Fire, born when lightning (his father) struck a tree (his mother). Others became bad guys, such as Surt, who was also a god of Fire. Some were friendly to the gods, such as Mimir and his daughters, the Norns. Others were the enemies of the gods, such as Thrym. It would have served no purpose if there were, for instance, two gods with authority over the same element.

In the same original pantheon as Loki were Skadhi, the winter goddess; Thjazzi, a master artisan, Ran, the goddess of the sea, and Aegir, her husband, the god of the sea. It is possible that Rig/Heimdal and Sif, Thor's wife, were also part of this ancient pantheon. Rig organized the race of Man into classes. Sif fulfilled the role of Vegetation Goddess.

In true Norse fashion, the peoples of the North set out to account for these elder gods and incorporate them into a new mythology, thus, lending credence to the Aesiric mastery of Midgard. Loki became the friend of Odin through blood-pact and was allowed live in Asgard under Odin's protection (*Lokasenna 9*). The only god Loki was in fear of was Thor.

Skadhi became the wife of Njord, after the hostage exchange and therefore the stepmother of Freyja and Frey (*see Skirnismal*). Aegir became the owner of the largest cauldron for making mead (this being the sea) and remained as a god of the sea, though Njord presided over the prosperity of the sea.

Some of these elder gods became the mothers, fathers, second spouses and foster parents of the Aesir and Vanir. The list is too long to account for here. The point is that lineage is very important to the Norse and this idea is reflected in the geneologies of the gods, as well.

The offspring of these beings followed the social hierarchy of the people in a simplified way: Males became gods, whose mothers were Jotn but whose fathers were gods. Females became goddesses by marriage to a god. Hence Gerd, though of totally Jotn descent, became a goddess by marrying Frey. Skadhi and Sif became goddesses through marriage, while Ull was counted among the gods because of his mother's marriage into Asgard. This was different than the 'normal' tradition and leads me to believe that there were special circumstances surrounding some additions to the Aesir. Redemption was a standard practice, promoted by the Skalds, who were keepers of the lore. Few of the Aesir had two parents who were also Aesiric. Most had one parent who was either of Jotn or Elvish descent.

MIMIR

Mimir has many names, including Mim and Nidi. He is usually counted among the gods of Asgard, but he is older and never resided there. His place is in the middle of the Underworld and his well feeds the middle root of Yggdrasil. He is known for his wisdom and was sent by the Aesir as hostage to the Vanir at the end of the war between them. When the Vanir did not trust the counsel of Hoenir, they cut off Mim's head and sent it to the Aesir. Odin preserved it in various magical ways that it would always be able to dispense wisdom. Then he placed it at Mim's well and consults with it, and has made sacrifice to it. Mimir's daughters are the Norns, which were born to him and his sister, Bestla.

NORNS

They are the three daughters of Mimir: Urd, Verdhandi and Skuld. They spin and weave the life of all things, gods and man. Even Odin is not able to overcome them, nor command them in any way. Theirs is a law beyond his authority and even he is subject to it. Verdhandi weaves the Wyrd of the present and Skuld weaves the Wyrd of the future.

Urd weaves the Wyrd of the past and has the most authority of the three. Her well waters the Southern-most root of Yggdrasil, in the Underworld. She is also known as Hel. She has full authority over the dead, who reside in her ream, Helheim.

SURT

Leader of the Fire Giants. He is the enemy of the Aesir and battles against them at Ragnarok, where he kills Frey with his own sword. His home is Muspelheim, in the South.

LIEKIN

Liekin is the daughter of Loki. She is misshapen, ugly and has authority over the dead who die the second death. They are sentenced to her realm, called Niflhel, or Misty Hel, not to be confused with Niflheim, which is where Ice comes from, far in the North.

Leikn has a second duty. This is to transport the dead to their final judgment. When performing this duty, she rides an ashen horse, which has three legs (See Additional Notes at back of book). As Christianity grew in influence, so did the fear of death outside 'Church Protection.' To bolster that belief, the Church, changed the personage of Hel (Urd) into something to be feared, ie; Leikn. Niflhel became less a place of mist and cold, but rather, it became synonymous with the Lake of Fire and torment in the bible.

FENRIR

The great wolf is one of Loki's children with the Jotn, Angrboda. When he was young, he lived inside Asgard and was cared for by the Aesir. As he grew, they became increasingly concerned that he would become a dangerous enemy. They tried to tie him up using various things and ultimately asked the Dwarves to help. The Dwarves devised a ribbon, which Fenrir was wary of. He asked the gods that one of them put his hand inside his mouth, to show trust. Tyr volunteered. When Fenrir realized that he could neither break, nor bite though the ribbon, he bit Tyr's hand off. Since that time, Tyr has been known as Tyr, the One-Handed. Fenrir kills Odin at Ragnarok. Vithar, Odin's son, kills him in return.

JORMUNGAND

Also known as the Midgard Serpent, or the Midgard Worm, is another of Loki's children with Angrboda. When Odin and his brothers created Midgard, they placed Jormungand as a border all the way around it. Hence the title, Midgard Serpent. He and Thor are sworn enemies and Thor nearly caught him, while out fishing with Hymir (until Hymir cut the line). Thor kills him at Ragarok.

NYDHOGG

The Nydhogg is a malicious serpent, who gnaws at the roots of Yggdrasil, attempting the destruction of the tree and, by extension, all of creation. He also guards the Nastrond (the Corpse Shore) which is the way into Niflhel. At Ragnarok, he opens up this way for the dead souls of evil folk to escape and join the battle. Here, he teams up with Fenrir to rend and devour living folk. Many have made the mistake of thinking he is the same as the Midgard Serpent. They are two different beings.

GULLVEIG/HEID

We know from Voluspasaga 21 and 22 that Gullveig is also known as Heid. The difference is that she is known as Gullveig in Asgard and as Heid by the women of Midgard she taught Seidh to.

There are two schools of thought on who Gullveig is. The first is that she was originally, Freyja's attendant, who learned Seidh from her and, in turn, taught it to 'wicked women.' The second school insists that she is the same as Aurboda (which also connects her to the names, Angrboda and Heid). This is a theory that was posited by Viktor Rydberg, who goes on for PAGES in his proving and explores some pretty dark alleys. Frankly, you're either going to love Rydberg's work or you're going to want to punch him in the throat.

24

Both schools agree that she is of Jotn descent. That clan of the Jotnir was friendly to the Vanir which is why her death is the cause of the first war.

HRYMTHURS

The name Hrymthurs means Frost Giant. They are a special class of Jotn, being the offspring of Bergelmir and are enemies of the Aesir and the Vanir.

Ymir's feet mated with each other and Thrudgelmir was born. He was monsterous in all respects. Without benefit of mate, Thrudgelmir bore Bergelmir, who became the first of the Frost Giants. Their original home is Niflheim.

At Ragnarok, they lead the battle against the gods. Hrym comes from the East and holds the whole world in storm. Many people die because of this. It is interesting to note that weather patterns generally move from West to East. Therefore, a great storm coming from the East would be out of the ordinary and may be one of the signs of the end.

THRYM

In Old Norse, the word *Thrymja* means Thunder. He was an elder god of Thunder and Weather. In many respects, he and Thor had parallel authorities. While many Jotn became associated with the Aesir, Thrym became an enemy. He stole Thor's hammer and would only give it up if he were given Freyja as his bride. Thor disguised himself as Freyja and got Mjollnir back by slaying Thrym.

Thrym is the father of Thjazzi, who, in turn, is the father of Skadhi. This accounts for Skadhi's estate being known as Thrymheim. It was the family estate.

THIAZZI

Son of Thrym and eventual becomes head of that family of Jotns. He is the father of Skadhi. He is a shape shifter and a master artisan. Thiazzi and Loki have a tenuous relationship. He enlisted Loki's help to kidnap Idun to make her his bride. Loki also killed Thiazzi and bragged about it to Skadhi. His death is the reason Skadhi came to Asgard to seek revenge or weregild. It was Loki's idea to marry her to one of the gods, when she was tricked into choosing Njord as husband.

ANGRBODA AND AURBODA

Skirnismal 6 and Voluspa hin Skama 3 both give the names of Gerde's father as Gymer and Voluspa hin Skama 3 also gives her mother's name; Aurboda. Lokasenna 42 clearly states that Frey gave his sword as a betrothal gift to the Jotn (This would have been to Gerde's parents). Voluspa 39-40 states that Frey's sword is in the hands of Angrboda when Fjalar comes to get it at the outset of Ragnarok.

To futher bolster this opinion, both Angrboda and Aurboda have a shepherd that sits upon a mound (*Skirnismal 10-11 and Voluspasaga 41. Eggther, by name*). This would be a 'little thing,' if it weren't so glaring in its coincidence. Since there is no intermediate literature stating that Agrboda received the sword from Aurboda, we have to assume that they are one and the same person.

As Angrboda, she is the mother of many of Loki's monster children and is the sworn enemy of the gods. As Aurboda, she was also in Freyja's retinue and taught Seidh to her, thus making Freyja the goddess associated with that magical tradition.

26

ELVES AND DWARVES

Over the years (read; centuries), people who study such things have come nearly to blows over the subject of Elves and Dwarves. Are they different races of beings? Are they the same? Are they earlier pantheons of gods, or were they deified later?

In the words of Vizinni, "Go back to the beginning." Elves and Dwarves were created as maggots which hatched on Ymir's dead body. They, according to the Creation Story, were changed into a more pleasing form by Odin, Vili and Ve. So far, so good. We have the names of two races of beings, created at the same time. The confusion comes in because there are two names given: Elf and Dwarf. They must be two distinct races.

What adds to the confusion, however, is the different designations; 'Light Elves and Dark Elves,' and 'Dwarf and Black Dwarf.' We also know that BOTH are considered the creative artisans of nature in the mythology, ie; Brisingamen, Sif's golden hair, smithing, architecture, and more. But, the confusion, itself can also give us our answer. Stay with me, now. In Dvergatal, we have given the name of the king and ruler of the Dwarves as Motsognir. If we assume that this is a proper name, we get no closer to a solution. And, since that word shows up nowhere else but here, confusion is not resolved. However, if we consider that Motsognir is NOT a name, but an epithet; a nickname or kenning, we have a key to finally answer this question. Motsognir (or, Modhsognir) means 'mead-drinker' or 'mead-sucker.'

In Voluspasaga 28, we are told that it is Mimir, who drinks his mead of creativity every morning. In fact, according to this verse, he drinks it from Odin's sacrificed eye (here, called Fjolnir's Pledge). We also know that Mimir was the original owner of the Mead of Creativity and Wisdom. Mimir is the ruler of the Dwarves. "Modhsognir" is a kenning. This connects Mimir to the Dwarves – the creative artisans of nature – but this does not finish answering the question.

There are four personages attributed to the creation of the Brisingamen: Alfrikk, Dwalin, Grer and Berling. I can only find one reference to Gerr and Berling in one saga; Sorla Thattr, compiled by two Christian monks in the 14th century. So, let's deal with the first two only. First, it is a relatively new idea that the Brisingamen was made by the Dwarves, alone. The older version

27

of the story has it being made by Dwarves and Elves, together (at least now, we can account for an artisan named Alfrikk –meaning 'King of the Elves').

Ok..second element (I promise to tie all this together at the end. No cheating, now) is found in Havamal 143 where Odin gave runes to the Dwarves through Dwalin and to the Elves through Dain. We know that Dwalin is, therefore, of the Dwarf race and Dain of the Elven race. Alfrikk -- also spelled Albreich – figures prominently in the Neibelung Cycle as a treasure-hungry smith and king. Back to Dvergatal, which lists names that are specifically Elven: Dain, Gandalf (wand-elf) Vindalf (wind-elf). Next to Dwalin's name is the name Althjof, which has the same meaning as Alfrikk/Albreich (high- elf or Elf King). There is an old German tradition that says that there were TWO Alfrikks (Albreichs); father and son. Thidrek's Saga of Bern calls Alfrikk the Younger a Dwarf. This is the same personage as Althjof in Dvergatal. So…why is the 'king of the Elves' listed separately in Dvergatal? 1) to distinguish between father and son (Modhsognir – Mimir and Althjof – Alfrikk the Younger) and 2) to tell us that Dwarves and Elves are the same race and Mimir is their king.

Based on this, it is my opinion that we may have lost an epic amount of skaldic material, which may give an account of a civil separation between the Elves and the Dwarves. They are each one, part of the same race. But the separation may have come very early, since, by the time the creation story is handed down to us, they are already distinct.

ELVEN RACES
The Elven Race/Elven Clan is friendly to the gods; Van and Aesir alike. They are descended from Ivalde, who had two sets of three children, each (no, I'm not going to give you the whole genealogy. Breathe easier.) He had two wives; the first was the Jotn, Greip. She bore Three sons, Egil, Voland and Slagfinn (yes, this is the same Voland, the great smith). The second wife was an unnamed Sun Dis in some of the mythologies and in others; she is Groa (the same Groa who is also mother to Svipdag/Od). One of her daughters with Ivaldi was Idun.

Since we have established that Elves and Dwarves are the same race, we know that they are the master artisans of nature. Egil is the artist who invented skiing. Voland is the great smith, later

28

deified and worshipped by peoples throughout Europe. But, of the three Elf-princes, only Egil may have remained friendly to the Aesir.

Here, I must say that attempting to put together an accurate genealogy of the Elves is next to impossible. Names like Thjazzi, Orvanedel, Groa, Idun and the relationships between them and others crop up only to confuse us all. Don't try it. That way lies madness.

Egil

He is also called Orvindel by Saxo Gramaticus. His brothers are Volund and Slagfin. Egil was a great warrior who often traveled with Thor in his raids upon Jotnheim. He was the husband of Sif and the father of Ull. Egil is also the father of Od/Svipdag by Groa, though we do not know whether this was before or after the birth of Ull. Egil is the inventor of Skiing, Archery and Skating.

Volund

The great artist and metal smith. This fact, in and of itself, is proof that Elves are not averse to Iron or any other metal. Various spellings of his name include Weyland. Some traditions count Volund a deity of great antiquity. The Norse, however, gives his genealogy as Elven (*Volundarkvida 14 and 35*). In fact, he is a prince of the Alfr, and one of the chief reasons I believe that the Alfr are an earlier pantheon of deities. Though Volund's race and family is friendly to the Aesir, he has been treated shamefully by them and hates them.

Delling

The father of Dag (Day), he is the dawn. Delling is the guardian of Briedablik, the home of Baldur and Nanna. He also opens up the day with a prayer of blessing (see section on Prayers and Songs).

Dain

We know very little about Dain from the literature. He is, however mentioned prominently in the Havamal receiving Runes for the Alfr from Odin.

DWARVES

The Dwarf race was created at the same time as the Elves (see section on Elves and Dwarves for more detail). They are master artisans of nature, building Breidablik as a home for Baldur and the Asmegir. They are also the guardians of the Underworld, especially Mimir's Grove, Odainsakr, which means 'Acre- of- the- not- dead.'

There seems to me no mention of them partaking in the fighting at Ragnarok. Voluspasaga 45 says that "Mimir's sons spring up, the downfall bodes." Then, in vs 47, it states "At the gates of their grots the wise dwarves groan.." The inference is that the Dwarves are protecting their home and king and do not join the open battle at Ranarok.

Dvalin

A dwarf of great wisdom. He is the son of Mimir and one of the best artisans. Dvalin brought rune lore to the dwarves and was one of the artisans of the Brisingamen, as well as the cursed sword, Tyrfing.

Andvari

A dwarf artisan, who worked with Dvalin on many occasions. He is also the warrior who guarded the treasure of Volund (the Nibelung Treasure), which was taken by Loki to pay weregild.

Alfrikk

Alfrikk's name means 'King of the Elves.' He is also a son of Mimir (see pag 43) and therefore Dvalin's brother. Alfrikk is one of the four Dwarves who fashioned the Brisingamen. His name is one of the reasons there is so much confusion as to the distinction between Alfr and Dvergar.

Berling and Gerr

These two are mentioned infrequently and only in connection with the making of the Brisingamen. Since we know that many beings had more than one name, we might assume that we know them by something other than these two names. No one, to my knowledge, has ever taken the time to make such a connection, however.

OTHER LEGENDARY BEINGS AND ARTIFACTS

EINHARJAR

These are great human warriors who have been slain in battle. They are chosen by Odin on the field, during the battle. They reside at Valhalla, where they spend their evenings feasting and drinking and their days in combat and contest. At Ragnarok, they will come forth as part of Odin's Army against the enemies of the gods.

VALKYRJES

There is much confusion about the Valkyrjes. They were young women of noble birth (daughters of kings are mentioned most frequently in the Eddas). It is my contention that this classification may have been a warrior cult on the same order as the Berserkers, but of women only, like the Amazons.

The Valkyrjes are literally battle-maids. The existence of this cult and their prowess on the battlefield might very well have given rise to the Skalds giving them such a place of honor as to be received into Valhalla to serve ale at the feasts. It would stand to reason that the human Valkyrjes were dedicated to Odin and were formidable opponents in battle, just as the Berserkers were.

Contrary to a common misconception, the Valkyrjes are dedicated to Odin, not Freyja. They are given honor, by the Skalds, who wrote that the Valkyrjes serve mead in Odin's hall. As such, they became supernatural beings, rather than a mere mortal warrior cult. But they reside with Odin at Valhalla, not in Sessrumnir with Freyja. Voluspasaga 30 says "for thus are hight Herjan's maidens." 'Herjan' is ON for 'warrior' and is one of Odin's many names. But, this verse even lists the names of [at least some of] them: Skuld, Guth, Hild, Gondol and Gierskogul. We have another list of names in Grimnnismal 37, which adds to this Valyrje names we already know. Sigurdrifa was taken out of the battlefield by Odin, not Freyja. Had she been dedicated to Freyja, it would have been that goddess' responsibility, not Odin's.

BERSERKERS

Literally means 'the Wearers of the Bear Shirt'. The Berserkers were a separatist cult of warriors dedicated to Odin. They were shape-shifters, who went into an altered state of consciousness, during battle. There is speculation that their altered state of consciousness was induced by eating Amanita mushrooms. They were sought after to join bands of Vikings. It was considered good luck to have them on your side and bad luck if they were joined against you.

ASMEGIR
Literally means 'Kindred of the gods.' The Asmegir are two people, Hlif and Hleifthrasa, who reside with Baldur in safety until after Ragnarok. They are the new parents of the human race to repopulate the earth. Their names mean "Life" and "He who is persistent in leaving after death." (see Additional Notes at the end of the book) The Asmegir are mentioned many times in the old tales, however, not as often in the compendium of the Codex Regius. In Vafthrudnismal 44-45, Odin does ask Vafthrudir the direct question; "Who will repopulate the earth, after the Fimbul Winter?" The answer is just as direct: "Hlif and Hleifthrasa."

SLEIPNIR
This is Odin's eight-legged horse. He can run on land or in the sky. Odin rides him often, but most famously, during quest against of the witches at the yearly Wild Hunt. He was given as a gift to Odin by Loki, who is his mother.

BRISINGAMEN
This is Freyja's necklace. It is both powerful and extraordinarily beautiful and is supernaturally made by a team of both Elves and Dwarves. After it was made, Heimdall, in the form of a seal, fought Loki for it and ultimately won. He then, returned it to Freyja.

The existence of the Brisingamen in Norse literature is important. A necklace with divine connections is an archetype that shows up in many cultures around the world, in one way or another. To cite a few examples, there is the Necklace of Harmonia in Greek Mythology, the Necklace of the Lady of the Lake in the Arthurian mythology, Yakasani no Magatemas in Japanese mythology and many more. I could even include how the Loon got its necklace from Native American mythologies.

Mjollnir

This is Thor's war hammer. He carries it when he does battle against the Jotn and other forces who seek to destroy the gods or the gods' interests. Originally, in the literature, Thor's hammer was stone and was broken in a battle with the Jotn, Thrym, and was replaced with an iron one made by the Dwarves.

Hamingja

Each one of us has a Hamingja that is with us from the time we are born to after we leave this earth. This is not a conscience, which tells us whether we're doing something right or wrong. It records everything we do or say and speaks for us at the Judgment Seat of Hel. In essence, then, it is more of a Paraclete who defends us, if possible. Those of us who are deemed unworthy to enter Helheim have our Hamingja taken away from us and replaced by a second Hamingja, more suited to our character. The souls, then, are banished to Niflhel to await Ragnarok and the last battle.

Myrk-Riders

This term is commonly translated as 'the witches.' These are the followers of Gyf and magic users who the Aesir feel countermine their authority. These are the witches that Odin hunts in the Wild Hunt. Before you make a decision on that, please read pg 130 on the X Rune.

There is another theory postulated about them, that the Myrk-Riders are Idun and her sisters, the Swan Maids, seeking their husbands in the Wolfdales. The idea becomes too incestuous for me to wrap my brain around. Frankly, I do gravitate toward the first idea, anyway (*see Volundarkvida 1-6*).

33

34

NORSE VIEW OF CREATION

The world is created on the great Ash Tree, Yggdrasil. At the base of the tree is the Underworld, where the roots are fed by three life-giving wells. In that Underworld, lays Vanaheim; the home of the Vanir, Alfheim; the home of the Elves, Hel and Niflhel. In the lower branches of Yggdrasil is Midgard, which is the Earth, as we know it. In the highest branches is Asgard, the home of the Aesir.

In all, there are nine worlds, connected by Bifrost Bridge. They are:

Midgard .... the home of men
Asaheim .... the home of the Aesir
Vanaheim .... the home of the Vanir
Alfheim .... the home of the Light Elves
Svartalfheim........... the home of the Dark Elves
Jotnheim................. the home of the Giants
Helheim .... the realm of the dead
Muspelheim .... the realm of Fire and Heat
Niflheim................. the realm of Ice and Cold

YMIR AND THE UNDERWORLD

At the base of Yggdrasil and under it, lies the Underworld. Many realms comprise it and all beings came from it, or were created by beings that came from it. The Jotns were the first beings.

The first and oldest was Ymir. All created things spring from him, but he did not create all things. The second creature was the Great Cow, Audhumla. She nourished Ymir with her milk, but needing nourishment herself, she licked the salty ice. In so doing, a man's shape was revealed. This was the Jotn, Buri, who became the father of Bor, the father of Odin and his brothers, Hoenir and Lodur.

The nourishment Ymir received from Audhumla caused him to progenerate different races and beings. Under his left arm grew two beings and as brother and sister, they were born, Mimir and Bestla. From them came a handsome race, friendly to the gods: Urd and her sisters, Verthandi and Skuld. These three spin the wyrd of each person born in creation; deity and human alike. Verthandi spins the wyrd of Present. Skuld spins the wyrd of future. It is Urd, however, spins the wyrd of the past. As such, death is in her realm and authority. She has another name, ancient and revered. It is Hel. Hel's realm is one of bliss, not torture and destruction.

The dichotomy between Hel, as the Norse understood her, and death being a terrible thing shows the influence of the Church. Though Christianity took ideas from the Norse/Germanic mythology, those ideas were changed to support a fear of death outside of the sanctions of the Church. Hel's kingdom became a place of torment and destruction, which they equated to Sheol and the biblical "Lake of Fire." To do so, they had to change the idea of Hel, herself.

After the influence of Christianity, Hel was associated with Liekin, the daughter of Loki. She is the Dis of Disease and all diseases spring from her. She brings harm and destruction. She cannot be bargained with, but she can be defended against, and she can be fought.

Liekin also has another duty when one dies. It is her job to transport the dead to their final judgment before the gods on her three-legged horse.

Back to Ymir, whose progeny are still forming. His feet mated, one with another and from this union came Thrudgelmir. Thrudgelmir bore Bergelmir without the benefit of mate. This was the beginning of the Hrymthursi, or, Frost Jotns, a race formidable and unfriendly to the gods. It may be interesting to note that not all Jotns are ugly and misshapen. Some are incredibly beautiful, such as Gerd, who became the wife of Frey, and Skadhi.

Bestla, the sister of Mimir, was joined to Bor, the son of Buri. From this union came three brothers: Odin, Hoenir and Lodur (Ve and Vili). Odin became the father of the Aesir and, according to some accounts, from Hoenir and Lodur come the Vanir.

The World Tree, Yggdrasil, has three main roots in the Underworld. The Northern root is watered by Hvergelmir Well (primal life force). The Central root is watered by the Well of Mimir (wisdom). The Southern root is watered by Urd's Well (the Well of Fate) Urd's well is also known as the Power of Earth.

In the East of Underworld lies Alfheim. Close by is Briedablik (the home of Baldur while he is not allowed to return to Asgard or Midgard. This is also the home of the Asmegir (Lif and Liefthrasir). They are under protection until Ragnarok, when they come forth to become the new parents of mankind, after the destruction of Midgard. In the West is Vanaheim, the home of the Vana-gods.

In the North lies Niflhel (lit. Misty Hel) which is under Leikin's rule. Niflhel is a place of torment, punishment and final destruction. Hel is a place of peace and is ruled by Hel (Urd). Separating Hel from Niflhel is a range of mountains called the Nidafjoll (Nidi's Mountains).

CREATION OF MIDGARD

Odin and his brothers set out on a quest to rid what would become Midgard, of the Jotns who inhabited it. This meant dealing with their own family, as they too, come from Jotn stock. They destroyed Ymir, their great grandfather and from his ruins made Midgard a paradise. This is the earth, as we know it.

Ymir's body and part of his blood became the Earth; the coagulated blood becoming fertile soil. The rest of the blood, they gathered up to fill Ginnungagap, forming the seas. His bones were used to form the mountains.

Maggots became evident in the decaying body and these they transformed into the Elves and Dwarves.

SIX ELEMENTS OF MAN

I mentioned earlier that the Norse tend to not reinvent the wheel (so to speak) whenever possible. The creation of Man was no exception. Odin and his brothers took two trees, Ask and Embla (Ash and Elm) and fashioned them into man and woman, respectively.

At man's creation, he was composed of six elements. Four of the six were gifts supplied by Odin Vili and Ve.

Spirit	the gift of Odin
Soul	the gift of Hoenir

Litr	Lodur's gift (the inner body, the light, formed in the image of the gods)
Blood	Lodur's gift (transformed from the sap of the tree)
Power of Growth	found in Ask and Embla
Earth Matter	found in Ask and Embla, born by Hoenir's winged servants to those who would be mothers.

Litr is the inner body. It is formed in the image and likeness of the gods. The appearance of the body (Earth Matter) is dependent on the Litr. If the Litr is beautiful, the body is also beautiful. If the Litr changes, the body changes.

Mortal death means that the Blood, Power of Growth and the Earth Matter separate from the Spirit, Soul and Litr. The latter three compose the person who is taken to the Underworld. For a time, then, there is a Doppelganger. This is what we know as a ghost. The ghost has more to do with the strength of the soul and its ties to this earthly realm. When we help someone cross over from this life, it is putting that soul to rest. This completes the separation between the former three elements and the latter three.

Crossing someone over does not involve making intercession before the gods for him or her, to insure a peaceful afterlife. This is one of the duties of the person's Hamingja – sort of a guardian angel – who also speaks for the departed at their judgment and prepares their place in Hel.

The Soul can be fed in various ways, which is why some ghostly manifestations can be experienced for years or even centuries. This ghost (from the German, Geist, which means spirit) should not be confused with the spiritual legacy of the person. Many times we can feel a presence, but it is not the person's soul we feel, it is the legacy within a particular object or place that had meaning to the soul, while alive.

If one is doomed to die the Second Death, it means that his Hamingja has been taken away from him. His soul is, then, separated from his Litr. The soul, receives a second Litr corresponding to its condition at death. At this, the person's soul is sent to Niflhel, beyond the Nidafjoll Mountains, which is the place of destruction and torment, usually associated with the Christian hell.

The Second Death is a special condemnation reserved for those who were particularly evil in this life. Eirick the Red might not have been condemned to this Second Death, where a person on the order of Vlad the Impaler (from the propaganda, not, necessarily the true Vlad) would have most likely been sent to Niflhel. Just because someone kills another person does not condemn him to the Second Death. This decision is made by Hel and not by mortal men or the gods.

It is interesting to note that death is not a judgment reserved for man by the gods. The Norns' decision on lifespan takes precedence over the authority of the gods. The judgment of the gods is only what to do with that person after the Norns have made their decision.

Because the authority of the Norns is not subject to Odin and the deities, the deities, themselves, are not exempt from it. In other words, the gods can die. They can also grow old, as witnessed by the saga of Idun's kidnapping. She is in charge of dispensing the Apples of Youth to the gods, which keep them young and strong. When Thiazzi kidnapped her, to be his wife, the gods started to grow old until she was rescued and brought back to Asgard.

One reason why songs, sagas and stories are so important is that, by singing the songs and telling the stories, that person (or deity) was still alive. The greater the deeds, the greater the songs. The greater the songs, the more strength of life the person (or deity) has. Eternal life is a foundational belief in many ancient cultures and the Norse are no different. Death, then, is not considered final.

In our culture, we are not accustomed to comprehending authority above deity. Nor, are we taught in our culture that gods are not eternal. But in the old traditions, this was so. Death, then, had slightly different meaning than what we have been brought up with. Death, for man, is a removal from active, participation, in tangible form, from Midgard.

39

THE BEGINNING (AND END) OF THE WORLD

The story of the First War is found in the *Voluspasaga*. It tells of how the Aesir are challenged by Gulveig, a lone Jotn, whom they could not kill and the result was a full-scale war between the Aesir and the Vanir. The two pantheons nearly annihilated each other before they made peace and exchanged hostages, in an effort to keep that peace.

Voluspasaga also gives passing reference to the creation of the world as well as the roles and relationships between some of the deities. The lack of detail is very important, here. It assumes that the listeners were already familiar with a more full understanding of these events and it was unnecessary for the Skald to relate them. He would only have to refer to them to give credence to the song.

At the risk of sounding euhemeristic, I have a theory that the story of the First War mythologizes the wars between the migratory tribes and those who had already settled in what became known as Scandinavia. Historical accounts may be lost (for various reasons) but we still have the 'gods' perspective' of those wars. If this were true, it would also account for the redoubled efforts of the Skalds in assimilating the mythologies into one semi-contiguous whole.

There has been a fair amount of controversy over *Voluspasaga* and especially the account of Ragnarok contained therein. Some historians believe that it is merely an account of the coming of Christianity to Scandinavia in earnest in the 9th and 10th Centuries.

Others point to the antiquity of certain verses and ideas, which predate the coming of Christianity.

The story of Ragnarok, and, for that matter, the whole of the *Voluspasaga*, does not allude to the coming of Christianity. Those who assume such have made the grave mistake in believing that Judeo-Christianity is the only philosophy which has ever suggested that there would be an end to the world, as we know it. Across history and across the world there are similar stories of the end of an age or the destruction of the Earth. The Norse were no different. In fact, it is quite possible that the accounts of Ragnarok and the Christian Apocalypse have the same Indo-Persian root. This is not

41

as far-fetched as one might think. Many of the Norse and Greek myths, such as Baldur and Hod, or even the Ascent of the Gods from primordial roots come from the same archetypes and grew up simultaneously with the stories of the Titans and the Olympian gods.

Ragnarok is usually translated "The Twilight of the Gods." It is more aptly translated the "Storm of Powers." It is the final war between the forces of evil and the forces of good. Nobody comes out unscathed, gods and old gods, alike.

THE FIRST WAR

After the worlds were formed and Midgard was cleared of the Jotns, the Aesir sat back to enjoy themselves on the Udall Plains. It was a time of peace and recreation and a time to build a great fortress to live in. Not that they were in any danger from enemies, but this fortress of the gods – known as Asgard – would also show their greatness.

Now, let us jump ahead in the story. Asgard is built in all its glory. Temples and altars are raised to the Aesir and the Vanir were not happy about it. They sent a Jotn, friendly to the Vans –she who was called Gullvieg - to provoke the Aesir into a war. As far as the Vans were concerned, there should only be one pantheon of deities worshipped. The Aesir had other ideas, so they killed Gullvieg. She refused to stay dead. So they killed her again. In fact, they killed her three times and she would not die.

Peace talks between the Aesir and the Vanir broke down and this was enough to incite the Vanir into attacking the great fortress of Asgard. When the Vans approached in battle array, Odin took his spear and threw it over the heads of the opposing army. This was the first act of war. With Njord in the lead, the Vans broke down the gates of Asgard and all out war ensued.

Though no account that I have read tells of any deities dying in that fight, both sides knew they were in danger of annihilating each other. In other words, no one would win in the end. So, the gods took counsel together and decided for peace between them. Hostages were exchanged to insure peace. It was agreed upon that Hoenir and Mimir would be sent to Vanaheim as counselors and Njord, Frey and Freyja would be sent to live in Asgard. From that time on there has been peace between the Aesir and the Vanir.

42

Though the Vanir are great warriors, their offices have more to do with prosperity and growth. The Aesir, on the other hand, lean more toward protection and defense. Everybody won.

RAGNAROK

We actually know fewer details about the First War than we do about Ragnarok, the final battle of the ages. But whether this is a continuation of all wars from first to now, or a wholly new fight is open to conjecture. Voluspasaga seems to indicate that one event led to another; from the First War on through the death of Baldur and the Fettering of Loki. Loki has broken his bonds and has come to seek revenge on the Aesir and the Vanir. He is bent on the destruction of all things and, though the text of Voluspasaga does not indicate this, it seems he means to be master of all.

Even the dead are divided. Those who now reside in Hel are at the side of Baldur and the gods. At Loki's side is his daughter Leikn, who has opened the gates of Niflhel. The dead are armed and ready to do battle. Those who enjoyed the peace of Hel are against those who are bent on destruction.

The Nidhogg Serpent and Fenrir, the great wolf, have teamed up. Fenrir rends the bodies of the dead and the Nidhogg devours them. The children of Fenrir break loose and one, Skoll, the worst of them all, swallows up the sun. Another, Hati, devours the moon. Now, there are cataclysmic weather changes.

Three cocks crow. Fjalar is bright red and his crowing wakens the Jotn. Gullinkambi has a gold comb and crows in Asgard. The third is dark red and is heard from Hel's halls. These three announce the coming of the final battle. Hrym and the Frost Giants attack from the east. Jormungand, the Midgard Serpent, rises from the water surrounding the Earth. Naglfar, the ship of the dead, sails south, captained by Loki, himself.

Surt, the Lord of the Fire Jotn surges northward out of Muspelheim. He does not care who might be in his way. Both friend and foe fall at his coming. Odin goes forth to battle Fenrir, while Frey battles his old enemy, Beli, whom he kills as Surt reaches them. Frey's sword is on its way, but it is in the hands of Surt, who received it from Eggther, the sword-watcher. The battle between Surt and Frey ensues and Surt kills Frey with his own sword.

43

Vithar joins his father, Odin in the fight against the wolf. The wolf kills Odin and Vithar avenges his father's death. Fenrir dies with Vithar's sword through his heart. Thor attacks his old enemy, the Midgard Serpent and kills him. With all the sorrow surrounding Frigg, this day, this is a source of pride to her.

The battle rages on, but is coming to a close with the death of Odin. Tyr slays Garm, the hound who guards the way to Hel, but he is so badly wounded that he falls. Heimdall kills his archenemy, Loki. The battle is so hard-fought between them that he too dies.

The Sun goes dark and the Moon sheds no light upon the Earth. No star can be seen in the heavens. The Earth is in flames and sinks down into the sea, but not forever. It rises from the sea, new, green and alive.

A new age begins for the world. And with a new age, new gods take over the old thrones. Baldur and Hodur return to sit in their father's stead at Valhalla. Magni and Modi assume the role of protector from their father, Thor. Hoenir returns to Asgard and brings the gift of foresight with him.

Hlif and Hleifthrasa, the Asmegir, return to populate the Earth. They no longer need the protection of Hel, Baldur and Dvalin. All who would have wanted them destroyed have passed out of existence. The Nidhogg carries the dead down into the depths of Hel, and the process of cleaning up the Earth begins with this age.

But, what of the Aesir and the Vanir as we know them? Njord returns to Vanaheim. His time of Hostage is over with the passing of the age. People have assumed that Thor dies in the battle with Jormungand. But Voluspasaga never says this. It does, however say that the Aesir have retired to their original home, the Udal Plains. The goddesses are not mentioned.

Do the Aesir and the Vanir, as we know them, take the historic role that the Jotn did? Do they become the 'new' old gods? If this is so, new deities will arise and have to prove their lineage back to the Aesir and the Vanir, just as they did with the Jotn. Now, will be a new age of sagas and songs to tell the stories of a new mythology.

44

GOVERNMENT AND SOCIETY

The type of government of any given nation or people is a two-way relationship. First, it reflects the culture's history. Whenever a need arose, a solution was necessary. The solution becomes a policy and the policy becomes tradition. Such things may be based on religious traditions, as well. The gods demand a certain form or order and the solutions to necessarily reflect that form. It is because of this that traditions, legal philosophy, custom, as well as system of government will look different in varying cultures.

But government performs a second function, too. That function is to maintain a status quo. The mandates of government are made to ensure that status quo for the future. This means that culturally acceptable punitive forms also become part of the mandate. For instance: a culture may feel that caning, flogging, or inflicting bodily harm is culturally acceptable for certain crimes against people or society. Another culture may accept amputation as punishment, or even slavery as warranted for the same crimes. Neither may see the need for execution. That may be viewed as too harsh a punishment. Yet a third culture may believe that execution should be the norm.

The legal philosophies of Western and Northern Europe had many similarities, but they also had many differences because the cultures were different. One of the things that fostered the similarities was that the Vikings were, in many ways, enforcers of tradition. The traditions that they learned from previously conquered tribes (please read as assimilated) spread with them as they continued on their way. Their philosophy of assimilation, rather than annihilation, helped to breed a homogeny among the tribes in Europe. Even today we can see cultural similarities when we compare the different European peoples to each other. On the other hand, we see possibly less similarity – in some respects – when we compare them to American culture. Why is that so, if our system of government, not to mention so much of our culture is rooted in Western Europe?

The answer is that we had different influences in our formative years than they did. One needs to look no further than the influence of the Iroquois Confederacy to see this. As a culture, the Iroquois had considerably less impact on Europe than they did on a fledgling, undeveloped United States. There were elements of the

Iroquois Confederacy's democratic style of government, however, which made perfect sense to the framers of the Constitution, though, because similar elements had been part of English culture to some extent for hundreds of years. It was because of those same cultural elements, too, that King John of England could comprehend the Magna Charta in 1215. He didn't like it, but he understood it.

Originally, all Norse family heads represented their own families and spoke for them. Alliances were based on kinship, first, then friendship or oaths and gifts. As the word of a man was most important, to be known as an oath-breaker was cause for offense. To be proven as such was cause for outlawry. But as clans grew, the responsibilities of Godi and Thingmen grew side by side and became more defined.

The local assembly of elders and judges was called the Thing. They were representatives who would convene and decide cases, pass judgment and recommend changes in law and custom. It was a completely civil, parliamentary body. Norway and Iceland were each split up into four districts and the Thing met for each particular district twice in the year. The first was held in the Spring, when local judgments were passed and decisions were made as to what should be presented to the Althing. The second time was in the Autumn, about eight weeks after the Althing. This meeting was simply to report what had transpired there.

Iceland had another part to its Althing, as well. Aside from the four districts "courts" they had a fifth court, which met during the Althing. This was a sort of Court of Appeals. All judgments of the fifth court at the Althing were final. The reasoning behind this additional judicial body was that Iceland had no king. There was no executive branch to carry out laws and decisions. The Lawspeaker was the final authority on what the law said and how it should be interpreted.

Though it seemed to work for four hundred years or so, it had a down side to it. It meant that the law was frequently taken into the hands of the people. This is where honor and family relationship showed itself most importantly. Compensation, either by revenge or weregild, was a duty that followed the same hierarchy as inheritance. In other words, it was one's sworn and customary duty to avenge a wrongful death in the family. And all deaths at the hand of another were considered wrongful.

Following the first few layers of inheritance and compensatory duty, the line of responsibility looks like this:

1. The father
2. The son
3. Brother of the father (paternal uncle)
4. Paternal Grandfather
5. Grandson (son's son)
6. Maternal Grandfather
7. Grandson (daughter's son)

There are more layers than this, but this gives you an idea as to who was in line for inheritance. You can also see how, in Shakespeare's Hamlet, the uncle could come to power so easily: If the uncle's brother was dead and Hamlet was deemed insane, he would be the next in line to the local throne. All he needed was the agreement of the Thing and it was so.

As far as revenge was concerned, having such an intricate system was one of the reasons it sometimes took so long to carry out. One might be wronged and want to seek revenge on someone who killed a next of kin, but who's responsibility was it to do so? It may be someone else's, like an older brother's or a grandfather's responsibility before it falls to you.

MIGRATIONS

There are five main reasons why a tribe may migrate from one place to another: Natural Catastrophe, Aggression, Religious Beliefs, Economics/Access to Resources and Culture. Some of these reasons may compound, thereby supporting the need to migrate. A prime example, from a more contemporary period, would be the Mormon Church. They were victims of persecution at the hands of the mainstream Christian denominations. I put that persecution into the category of 'aggression.' At the same time, they embraced a religious prophecy, which promised them a land of their own, where they could live and worship in peace and safety.

Some tribes, on the other hand, are more culturally driven to a migrational lifestyle: The Saami, Bedouin, Romanii and many First Nation tribes are good examples of nomadic cultures and history. With them, I also see the overlap of Access to Resources. I'm sure we can all think of many more examples.

I believe that the ancient Proto-Norse peoples fell into three out of five of these categories supporting migration. I find no system of prophecy or religious belief, which would indicate that they sought a land to which their gods would lead them. So, we'll eliminate that one, right off the bat. The subcultures of the Proto-Norse were not ones which lent themselves to migratory shift, or a migratory lifestyle. They were well- settled between the Rhein River area, The Danube River and the Baltic Sea, and saw no real need to change that. They would have to be driven out.

Least important of the three reasons for their migrations was 'economics.' They had ample access to resources to sustain their culture right where they were. They did not follow herds of Reindeer or Horses and had ample access to food, water and shelter. Therefore, Economics became more of a supportive reason for going north. Economics may have given them a direction to go, but was not the driving reason for leaving.

Also in the Rhein Valley and to the west, were nations of Celts. In fact, there is an old adage that one was considered Celt or Norse depending on which side of the Rhein his family came from. There was much contact between the two, both in trading and war. But this contact was not the invasion which drove both sides to leave the area. Enter the Romans.

The Romans embraced an expansionist philosophy and set out to be masters of the world. By the 1st Century BCE, they had entrenched themselves in what is now Germany and pushed the Franks, Burgundians and Celts west into Gaul. By the 2nd Century CE, tribes of Herulians and Langobards, Saxons, Danes, Jutes, Sviar, Goths, Vandals and pretty much everybody else, were pushed in all directions. Rome came down on the area like a big foot, scattering Proto-Norse tribes.

The period that we normally name the Viking Era is relatively short. The period of time between ca. 800 and 1100 CE was an era of great expansion for the Nordic Peoples. Explorations were undertaken. Trade was opened up. Wars were fought over many reasons. But it is difficult to separate this short period of time from the events leading up to it. The changes in culture and society were sometimes dramatic. The peoples of the north were not always a war-like race. Nor did they remain that way, after the 1066 CE and the Battle of Hastings. We commonly refer to this date as the end of the Viking Age.

I, however, refer to the Viking Age as lasting from circa 300 CE to ca. 1100 CE. This period includes some of the more dramatic migrations and cultural assimilations, which led into the 800's. We could go back further; even into the mythological and speculative roots of the race but the Migration Period of the 300's is a more logical place to start. By this time Roman Expansion into Europe was a foregone conclusion.

It is important to note that there were many migrations – in all directions – of the Norse and Proto-Norse peoples. We tend to think about the Sviar, for instance, as traveling north to Scandinavia and staying there. This is not the case, since they also migrated back south, then north again. Between the 2nd Century BCE and the 7th Century CE, there were as many as three major migrations of the tribes. Since I am concentrating on the tribes that are known to have settled in Scandinavia, there is a lot of material I have purposely left out of this book.

Tribes of Hermiones, Ingavones and Istavones had banded together as confederacies of common peoples with a common heritage. Mythologically, at least, the Hermiones (or, Irminones), Istavones and Ingavones were the three great 'original' peoples who developed into what we now refer to as Norse/Germanic. Some writers list as many as five 'original groups. Other writers list the Vandals and the Goths as parts of one of these three. The Teutons are descended from the Hermiones, where Germany gets its name. At that time there was also a more clear-cut designation between the Celts and these three great peoples. We are less sure of the descent of most other tribes, such as the Burgundians, Goths, Suebi and so forth. There is contradictory information on them. It is my personal belief, however, that the Sviar are descended from the Ingavones, in that the major collective was named for Ing (Frey), thus making them followers of the Vanir. I have yet to find anything that points in any concrete direction.

The formidable Burgundians had split in at least two of the major migrations; some going North with the Sviar, the Goths and the Saxons; others were chased into Gaul by the Romans, where they've settled ever since. Here is where we can count the division of the Sviar into the Swedes and the Saxons, who went North, then traveled West, finally ending up in the British Isles.

Through the Migrations, a couple of things happened in the religious understandings of the peoples. They were familiar with many deities already. Most of these took a smaller role in the life of the culture. Deities, who were more elemental in nature, were important to appease. Gods of Fire, Lightning, Rain and Hail, Winter and the like were the ones to worship. Deities of cultivated vegetation, such as Ostara, Sif and Idun, took a back seat, but were never forgotten. Instead, the Jotn – more elemental in nature- were revered.

Along the way, the migratory nations encountered other cultures with deities of their own. These were assimilated into the larger culture and worshipped along with the rest. Now we have a dilemma on our hands, as the new gods, the Aesir, promised protection from the old gods. The Jotn were eventually eliminated from worship, for the most part, and replaced with such deities as Odin and his brothers. To appease those who still followed the 'old ways', intermarriage was introduced as a solution. The Jotn were still looked at derogatorily (as time went on) but it solved the problem of how we got new gods to replace the old. The new gods were the children of the old gods. When migrating Istavonic tribes made it to what we now call Scandinavia, they found the Sviar had already settled there, having brought other remnants of their own basic belief structure with them.

Having temporarily left their own nomadic ways behind and taking up a more agrarian lifestyle meant that the Sviar no longer worshipped the same old gods, as well. Theirs was a pantheon, more dedicated to vegetation and the fruits of the Earth. These gods are the Vanes, who had been adopted the same way as the Aesir, but at an earlier time. Worship of the Vanir was entrenched in the north by the time other Nordic tribes arrived. It is because of this that the Eddas suggest that the Vanir are an older race of deities than the Aesir.

So, in the end, we had deities who had a much smaller role in the beginning, coming to the forefront and we had introductions to new deities. These were adopted to serve the current purposes of the culture. Between the two, we have a new race of deities taking over from the old.

As time went on, the culture of the people became more complex, to reflect the relationship of the gods to the people. On a more tribal level, intermarriage between enemies was seen as a solution to war. One does not make war against a brother. Nor does one take a brother's land. After all, if he is your brother, it is as much your land as his. But it also meant that his enemies were your enemies. If your sister was married to his enemy it meant that much negotiation needed to take place before peace could reign. It also meant the giving of gifts to make peace. Land, goods that reflected prosperity, or personal honor were all seen as negotiable tools. This was seen on a familial level, as well as tribal. And a hierarchy in the culture, not to mention the family, was born.

One god at the head of all (Odin) and deities with their own authorities under him (his sons, daughters, wives, to name a few) was a philosophy reflected in the tribes, and kingdoms. By now, the society was complex, socially and religiously. This complexity reflected the philosophy "as above, so below" or more accurately, "as below, so above."

But as the society grew, so did its needs. A common complaint was that the land was becoming too populated (this is not true by today's standards, but it was for them). Trading and piracy helped to fill those needs. In the process, strange ways and religious beliefs were also introduced to the North. That caused a violent reaction among those who hung on to the Old Ways. All this led up to the expansionist period we call the Viking Age between ca 800 and 1100 CE.

GROUP RELATIONSHIPS

This book is not meant to be an anthropological treatise. It is meant to be a study of the ancient ways and to bring them forward, adapting them to society, today. There has been too much desire for the ancient ways but not enough understanding of them. Many practices are recorded in sketchy terms, at best. But that hasn't stopped anyone from forming a new tradition out of it.

Group dynamics and relationships are very important, but the thing that seems to be missing in today's culture is the sense of patience and work that must go into it for it to flourish and grow. In most Pagan circles, groups are formed out of desire but they rarely stay together for any length of time. At best they become a fond memory quite quickly. More often than not, they become a bitter memory for those involved. The average life span of a working group, whether it is called a coven, church, hearth, Circle or family, is less than two years. This hardly gives any group a chance to mature. Don't get me wrong, individuals might grow but groups rarely do. I know of very few Pagan groups who have stayed together more than five years. Of those few, I know even fewer who have had no turnover in membership for that length of time. I am not speaking of adding new members. I am talking about people leaving the group.

Here is one of the problems. We read about the ancient ways and desire the magical power they speak of. More often than not, in history, those groups were formed out of a solid family bond and had that bond at the core of the magical relationship. In desiring what the ancients had we set out to form groups to explore/recreate what they experienced and were able to do. We read about them. We experiment with their methods and ideologies. But we forget a very important point: that what we are reading in a few pages may have taken years or generations to develop.

We live in a culture based on "bigger, better, faster, more." We want it all now. As a culture, we don't want to work for what they had; we want to have in a year what it took them a hundred to build. When things don't go the way we planned, we get disillusioned. Then, the infighting starts and that gives us our reason to walk away/disband/give up/look for something new.

We read about the amazingly powerful works that our ancient predecessors did. In many cases, these events might have been

55

years apart. But we read about them in a couple of pages or one paragraph and wonder why we can't do in a week what they did over twenty years. So we think that things are not going the way they were planned and we think that the gods have failed us. Or we think that they had some powerful secret that we don't have. We start to search for that secret; that thing that will make it all better and release the power of the Kracken that we know is pent up inside us. Then we start to think that maybe all the stuff we've read is only story and lie. We question the gods and question the motives of others in the group. We become suspicious that others are out to steal the wonderful abilities that we know we have inside us. Believe me, I've seen this happen in many groups; not only ones I've been involved with, and, it happens frequently.

The shame of it all is that you may very likely have the abilities that you think you have. And maybe everyone else in the group does too. But it is important to act out of the same patience you would have for a family member that you do with a coven member. It is important to act out of the same sense of protection, as well. What you desire may take years to build in the way that it is supposed to be built. That kind of foundation becomes a formidable strength and ability. It is one thing for someone outside your Circle to desire harm to you or your group. It is quite another to experience that concern from within.

And now we come to the subject of giving your word. No matter what ancient tradition you might currently be studying, you will most likely find that your word is your bond. If you read the philosophies of your pet ancient culture, you might find somewhere in there… hidden away…tucked into a whispered corner, that the only thing you really have, when all is said and done, is your reputation. That reputation is based on what your history is. That history is based, partly, on how you have given your word and how you have kept it. If you know you have a hard time giving an oath and keeping it, don't give it. If you know you cannot keep the secrets of your group, do the group a service and let them know you can't be trusted with certain types of information. This whole expression is based on the assumption that there is honesty at the core of your own being.

The other side of that sense of truth is understanding. This comes from a desire to protect those with whom you have made the bond. I have known cases where a member of a working group has gone to another and poured his heart out, only to have that information used against him. Instead of acting out of protection, such as one might do with a blood-family member, the second person opens the first up to a potentially damaging situation, making him vulnerable. Every member of a working group should be afforded the same sense of love and protection. This builds trust within the working group. That foundation becomes an ethic on which the working group can grow and become strong. There is no fear involved.

My final comment on this subject is; "Be careful with whom you make bonds of kinship." Do not give your oath freely, as it can come back to haunt you, putting you in a situation where you will have to act on that oath. Good working groups are built slowly and patiently, over time and the foundation remains intact.

CELEBRATIONS

At this time, we are only sure of the general times of the four major blots. There is information which may lead us to more (see Additional Notes), however, much archeological information has not been translated (which I find quite interesting) OR, if it has, it has not been made available to the general public.

That being the case, we can roughly assess when the major blots are held and work from there. Since there are any number of reasons why a group should hold a Sumbl, Feast or Blot, allow me to lay a foundation:

1) Any group is likely to have its Patron or Matron deity. Is there a time, during the year, when the season is more in keeping with that deity's nature? (Ex: Harvest time for Sif or Idun; Spring for Ostara or, possibly Baldur; deep winter for Skadhi or Ull). For that matter, is there a time of year, which has been shown to be important to a particular deity?

2) Are there yearly events in your group's keeping that could be precluded by a celebration to honor a deity? (Ex: Var, Baldur or Forseti before a Thing; Tyr or Odin before an annual war reenactment; Njord or even Thor before the annual fishing opener)

3) Are there groups or personages – or even EVENTS -- in the ancient writings, which you feel compelled to give honor to? (Ex: Valkjeries, Einherrier, Alfr, Odin's hanging on Yggdrasil,or Skadhi's storming Asgard and coming away with a husband)

4) Are there events within your group that are important to honor yearly, such as Rites of Passage or election of group officers (Hint: This would be a good time to hold an Inheritance, or, Ale Sumbl).

I have become increasingly concerned over the number of writers who claim they have all truth but never refer to historical documents to support their cases. Some of them have written some very imaginative works. There are others who only quote authors who, themselves, are quoting what someone else has written. It's like circular reasoning that goes like this: "This book is the truth. How do we know? The book says so." I'm afraid some of our favorite authors have played this game with their readers. It seems to me that if a writer is going to take the time to research material for a book, s/he should actually DO the research. It does his readership no good to only quote other contemporary writers without checking the source material.

There are so many contemporary authors who are attempting to prove the magico-religious practices of the Norse within a Wiccan framework that it boggles the imagination. Keep this in mind for now, as something I say later on might seem contradictory.

Wicca, as we know it, is not an ancient religion, unless you consider the 1940's ancient. Wicca is a synthesis of the ancient magical and cultural practices in Europe. Now, synthesis is not a bad thing, folks. Just because I use the word "synthetic" does not mean I am calling it "less than real." Wicca is a religion that works for many people.

The Calendar of Celebrations, which was first promoted by Gerald Gardner and others, is also a synthesis. It is a good calendar, true enough, and a logical one. But it is a calendar of celebrations synthesized from, primarily, the Norse and Celtic cultures of the ancient times. In other words, if you say you follow the Norse path exclusively, I can't envision you celebrating Beltane or Samhain, except as a cultural exercise.

The ancient ceremonial practices of the Norse peoples had nothing to do with that calendar. Nor, did their rites look anything like a Wiccan ritual. The problem is that we have little to go on for how most of those rites were actually performed. If a writer promotes an idea for ritual as a synthesis, this is good. He's being honest about it. But if a writer promotes his ideal ritual as steeped in history and therefore the "true ancient way," that writer is either deluded or only out for your money. Books of that sort make nice kindling. Enough ranting for the moment.

The Norse calendar was not lunar, meaning, keeping track of the phases of the moon and designing how the days of the year should be kept track of. They did, in fact recognize the phases of the moon, but their calendar(s) were not based on them. Nor, did it keep track of the Solstices and Equinoxes. In all of my research, I can find no system of astrology among the ancient Nordic peoples, as we understand astrology today. Astronomy was used as a navigational device and there are many ancient myths concerning the stars and constellations. But astrology did not exist as a practice that I can find. This should tell you one thing right off the bat; that Jul did not occur on the Winter Solstice.

BLÓTS AND SUMBLS

BLÓTS

Literally translated, Blót means blood. It was a ceremonial occasion, marked by ritual sacrifice of at least one animal. The blood was then used to bless the walls of the temple and consecrate it. After the temple was blessed, the people were consecrated in the same way, then the representations of the gods.

The process went like this: The animal was consecrated, then killed and the blood was collected into a copper bowl called a Blótbolli. The bowl was then taken before the gods and offered to them. With the use of the Blótkvist (blood twigs) the blood was splattered in the manner previously mentioned. This was all performed by the Hofgodi or 'house-priest'. The blood-spattering may have also been used for divination. This is alluded to in Hymiskvidha 1, where even the gods used such tools.

The Blót was not just a time of sacrifice. It was a gathering of the people, which included feasting as well. All were expected to bring their own ale as well as contribute food and resources for the feast. The main course of the feast was the sacrificed animal. After the blood was drained, the meat was cooked and served to the attendees. During the cooking process, there ensued much drinking of toasts and solemn vows. There was an order to the vows, which has been found in various sources. This leads me to believe that it was a fairly standard order. After the feast there would be a lot more drinking, till it was time to go....or fall over.

Blóts are also good times for divination. There is little I can find on the casting of the Blótspan, or, Sacrifice Chip. This was a wood chip dipped in the blood of the sacrifice. They would also cast lots for the same purpose, though I can find little as to the process here too. It seems to me that the casting of Runes would be an acceptable substitute for either of these two things. Look! A possible synthesis!

RITE OF THE SONAR GOLT

There was a particular order to the drinking of the horns at the Blóts. So, we know when the Rite of the Sonar-Golt, or Atonement Boar, was to take place at Midsvetrablót. This order will be covered later.

The men would gather round the boar and lay hands on it, making solemn vows. Then the Bragarkup would be drunk at the boar. The boar was then sacrificed in the usual manner. The meat would be consecrated and cooked over the fire, then served during the feast.

THE ORDER OF HORNS

There were five horns that were drunk at the Blóts, but only two were mandatory; the others were optional. Here they are in order.

1. To ODIN: For Victory and Power *(Mandatory)*
2. To THOR: By those who trusted in their own Strength and Power *(Optional)*
3. To NJORD AND FREY: For good years and peace *(Mandatory)*
4. To BRAGGI: When solemn vows, boasts and oaths are made *(Optional, except at the Julablót)*
5. To the ANCESTORS: This was a memorial toast and must be proposed by the Hofgodi *(Optional)*

To consecrate the horns before the Blót, the Hofgodi carried them around the fire, making the sign of Mjollnir over them. The meat was consecrated in the same way. The fires were considered holy at Blót.

SUMBL

A Sumbl is a feast to honor a particular deity, personage or event. But a Sumbl does not include a blood sacrifice. The Inheritance Feast, or Ale Feast, for instance, was a Sumbl to honor the son taking over authority and all household wealth from a father who had passed. He was, then, expected to give gifts to his supporters. He, in turn, was honored by them with much feasting and drinking.

The calendar on the next page denotes the difference between the blóts (called 'blóts') and the sumbls (called 'dags').

64

MAJOR BLÓTS THROUGHOUT THE YEAR

There are four important times during the year when a Blót would be appropriate for celebration. The dates are given in the contemporary calendar and are rough approximations based on comparing our contemporary calendar to the Icelandic calendar, developed in the 900's, that became a standard throughout Scandinavia. Each one of these four Blóts honors specific deities, seasons, or events, which are important to me.

One should keep in mind that there are only two seasons; Summer and Winter. Consequently, there are no Autumn and Spring festivals, per se. Since Vinternal was held in October, that would make (what we call) Autumn part of Winter. And, since the Sigurdsblót is also called Somerdag, that would make Spring part of Summer. I have also included notes on how I honor those things. You may have your own reasons for honoring those times.

In most of the family sagas I've read, there has been little to dissuade me that the Blóts they held for personal (or family) reasons did not happen at one of these four times. Other than returning safely home from a war or a harrowing journey, I have found little evidence to the contrary, if any.

One can hold a Sumbl for any reason to mark an occasion. Rites of Passage are a good reason to hold a Sumbl. If someone comes of age, if there is a marriage, birth or death in the family, these are all good reasons to honor the gods. Travel was hard, in the ancient days, so before embarking on a journey, or coming home safely, were reasons to perform a Blót. Thanking the gods by way of a gift of food or sacrifice is/was a standard way to honor them.

One king had a daughter who either ran away or was kidnapped (depending on the translation you read). When she was found, he called for month-long Blót (some texts say three days). This month was then named after her (Goi) and became part of the ancient Icelandic calendar.

I must day something here about ritual sacrifice at the Blóts. Our ancient predecessors did not see the Blót Sacrifice in the same way we assume, today; although their ancient predecessors did. The ritual slaughtering of animals was something that had fallen out of practice by the 800's (for the most part..not altogether). It was a tradition that slowly died away over the centuries. For that matter,

65

human sacrifice was -- even to the 'ancient,' ancient peoples – not something that was done on a regular basis. You'll find more examples of that in ancient Celtic tradition, than in the proto-Norse accounts. For more on this, I suggest you attempt to wade through the *Fornaldarsagur Nordurlanda.*The main problem with this collection is that the only version we have of these sagas (aside from the translations) was compiled by two Christian monks in the 13th century and the stories were dramatically Christianized. The real problem is in the keeping of the name, "Blót," which separated it from the Sumbls. Blóts are seen as a 'more holy' celebration; not, necessarily more solemn, but 'holy.'

JANUARY	
13	Jul/Midsvaetrablót
FEBRUARY	
6	Odinirveidhifor
MARCH	
15	Heimdalsdag
APRIL	
22	Ostara/Somerdag/Sigurdsblót
MAY	
2	Baldursdag
JUNE	
15	Midsomrblót
JULY	
AUGUST	
15	Freyjasdag
OCTOBER	
9	Leif Ericksonsdag
14	Vinternal/ Vaetablot/Disablót
NOVEMBER	
DECEMBER	

Here is a short explanation of each of the festivals listed above.

MIDSVAETRABLÓT   JANUARY 12TH - 14TH

Also called Julablót (Jul Sacrifice or Midwinter Sacrifice). The most important of all the yearly blóts. This was the hofudblót (chief sacrifice), a three- day event to ensure a prosperous year and peace. Vows are made to the gods, especially Frey, on the first night (Jul Eve).

Jul Eve is dedicated to Frey. Vows are made to him, blessings of abundance are asked for. The Rite of the Sonar-Golt (Atonement Boar) was performed on this night. The Swedes took time on this night also to mourn the death of Njord, for there had been prosperity and peace during his lifetime. I can find nothing on this, however. Vafthrudnismal clearly states that after Ragnarok, he retires to his home. In other words, he lives.

This is the most important celebration of the year. It is three days of feasting, magic, decision-making, bonding, sharing and divination.

As there is some confusion about whether the Julablot is different than the Midsvaetrablot (and there are sub-cultural answers to this question) it is easily solved. We set the first night apart as the Julablót, sacred to Njord and Frey.

Here, the traditional dinner would be the Boar. The Rite of Sonar-Golt is also performed on this night. Variations of this can take place, which do not include the sacrificing of animals. The Julablót also includes the Braggarkupp.

The second and third nights are good for divination, entertainment, story and song, spell work, feasting, bonding and camaraderie. The offering to the gods is given on the third night.

ODINIRVEIDHIFOR   FEBRUARY 6

This is Odin's Wild Hunt, where he seeks out the powers of darkness and scatters them to the four winds. This night can be marked by spell work to disperse negative forces in one's life; both internal and external. It is also a good time to revisit and strengthen any wards and protections on home, property, kith and kin.

HEIMDALSDAG   MARCH 15

Heimdall, also known as Rig, is the god who organized the classes of man: Thrall and Thir, Karl and Snoer, Jarl and Erna, and Kon. He also taught runes to Jarl and Kon. In this way he is responsible for man having runes of magic and divination.

Heimdallsdag is a time to honor those in our midst with rites such as Saging and Croning, elevations in group status and the deciding of authorities and offices.

The first few verses of Rigsthula actually give us a time frame for this sumbl. Verse 1 says that the earth was green, when he walked. We can, then, exclude the cold of winter. Verse 4 says that Edda fed him hardtack bread and soup made from calf meat. Since hardtack was a type of bread stored up for the winter and calves are born in the spring, Rigsthula is clearly talking about very early spring. This would put it in March (by our calendar) when the earth starts to go green again, but before the Sigurdblót, which usheres in the Summer.

SIGURDBLÓT/SOMRDAG   APRIL 22

Also called Somerdag. It is held at the beginning of Summer, around Mid-April (based on the two-season calendar), by the old reckoning (most likely around Ostara). This is a sacrifice to honor Odin for luck and victory. In ancient times, most wars, exploration voyages and trading expeditions were done in the early Summer, when the weather was better for travel. This is the second generally held Blót in the year.

BALDURSDAG   MAY 2

This is the day to celebrate justice and peace. It is a good time to usher in the time when disagreements are resolved. We strive to work together for the common well-being of the people.

In ancient times, Baldursdag would be held near or at the time of the regional Thing, or about 6 weeks before the Althing, which was held in mid to late June.

MIDSOMERBLÓT   JUNE 15

This was a time to take a rest from the work and make agreements for help with the work to come. Vows of loyalty and fealty marked the Midsomerblót. If a trader went out early in the Summer, he may come home at this time to make arrangements for the next campaign. The Blót was held partly to thank the gods for returning safely, and in part, for making new vows to the gods for the coming months.

The Midsomerblót was a big occasion at the Althing. All enmity was put aside. No feuding was allowed and no vengeance could be taken, unless one wanted to risk outlawry. During the Althing, judges decided suits, which could not be resolved at the regional Things. All this gives us the tone for celebrating the Midsomerblót. Since the Midsomerblót is held during the 2 weeks of the Althing. The vows you make to each other at Midsomer, therefore, become law.

Midsummer is a time celebrated by many ancient cultures. The Norse were no exception. This was a time to rest from the current work, sit back and say, "My crops look good!" It is a time for dancing, feasting, music and games. It is not a time to be complacent, however, but a time to prepare for the next step. Count your blessings, yes, but know what will be needed to bring the season to a fruitful end. What help will be needed? Who can you count on to help?

This is a good time for making agreements, solidifying relationships and vowing friendship and fealty. With this in mind, it is an excellent time for marriages.

FREYJASDAG   AUGUST 15

Consider that, as a time when warriors were returning from war and traders were returning home with much needed prosperity, this is a time to honor and thank Freyja for her help. Since prosperity is one of her offices, it is a good time to thank her for success. Returning warriors are in need of healing. And any day is a good day to honor love and sexuality.

Summer Day is the antithesis of Winter Night. Summer is welcomed in and we say farewell to Winter. This is a time to prepare the planting of crops and ask for blessings of growth. Frey, Frigg and Idun are important here. This is also a time for divination and asking for direction for the Summer months.

But the Summer was also a time when the kings went to war. Hence, it was also known as the Sigrdblót. To the ancients, this was the time when the 'trading and raiding' season begins. It is a good time to start new projects. Vows made during the Midsvaetrablót/Julablót are reviewed around the Horns. Again, the important Horns to drink are to Odin, Thor and the Ancestors. As at Vinternal, the Feast can also include entertainment, stories and songs.

But this can also be a time of judgment between brethren, using the model of the Thing. This event takes place back in the first sacred area before the Rite is ended in the usual manner, by offering a gift to the gods.

LEIF ERICKSONSDAG   OCTOBER 9
This is an official national holiday in the United States, but is not celebrated very widely. It commemorates the arrival of Leif Erickson as the first European to set foot on these shores.

VINTERNAL/VAETRABLÓT/DISABLÓT   OCTOBER 14
Also called Vetranacht (Winter Night) and Vetrablót. It includes great feasting and drinking. The cups and horns are consecrated to the gods. And all the Aesiric and Vanic goddesses were honored in the Blót.

Vinternal literally means Winter Night. Just as Summer is associated with the Day and the Sun, so Winter and its coming is associated with Night. Vinternal is a time to say goodbye to Summer and welcome the Winter. But this is not a time to say goodbye to the Day and welcome Night. Especially in the early Winter – mid-October through November – the season was spent preparing for the snows and cold weather; making sure houses could be kept warm, laying up food for household and livestock. This is the Harvest Time, so Vinternal is also a celebration of the harvest.

The celebration can include times of song and story, retelling the stories of the gods and heroes. It can also be a time to make things to bless the house and all therein. Remember, this is a celebration…And a feast.

It is here that the gods are called and invited to share in the feast. Here, too, is where divination is done, the Summoning of the Elements of Creation and the gift to the gods is offered.

70

Vinternal, due to its harvest aspect, is sacred to Frigg, Sif and Frey. The act of appeasing Winter Cold is in addressing Skadhi. Divination calls on the powers of the Vanir in general, as foresight is one of their gifts, or to Odin and the Norns when using the runes. Following the examples set in the Icelandic Sagas, the Vinternal is also a good time for marriages (*Vatnsdaela Saga 44 and Egils Saga 42-44*).

If the Horn is passed, this is a good time to boast about how Summer went and list accomplishments. The Horns to Odin, Thor and the Ancestors are important. After the Horns, the sacred area is exited for the second space, where the feast occurs. Horns and toasting can also be done during the feast if desired. Doing this has a great effect on the energy of the feast. In the second area, food, cups and fire are all made sacred by the sign of Mjollnir.

Ending the Rite takes place back in the first sacred space, where gifts of food from the feast are offered to the gods in thanks. This is also a time for giving direction, vows of support and acting on the divination and magic.

71

CALENDARS, TIMES AND SEASONS

Below are the months of the year as most of the ancient Norse saw it. It was by no means officially standard, but was accepted by many. There were other calendar systems to be found in Sweden, Norway and Denmark, some using a 19-day system. These were rather difficult to follow and it was possible for someone to say he was 18 years old when he was only 12 ½ (I'm exaggerating on purpose).

As a standard calendar was not set until sometime in the 900's, we have stories as to how some months were added to it. The month of Goa (mid-February to mid-March), for instance, was added when a king's daughter was kidnapped. They searched for a very long time and had nearly given up hope when she returned (I'm giving you the short version of the story). The king was so overjoyed that he held a 3-day Blót to thank the gods for her safe return and named a month at the end of the year for her.

Here is that Norse calendar and its correspondence to the standard calendar we use, today. I've given translations of month-names, whenever possible.

Norse Calendar	Translation	Contemporary Correspondence
Einmanudhur	First Month	mid-Mar to mid-April
Harpa		mid-April to mid-May
Stekktidh	Lamb-fold Month	mid-May to mid-June
Solmanudhur	Sun Month	mid-June to mid-July
Midsomer	Midsummer	mid-July to mid-Aug
Heyannir	Haying Time	mid-Aug to mid-Sept
Houstmanudhur	Harvest Month	mid-Sept to mid-Oct
Gormanudhur	Slaughtering Month	mid-Oct to mid-Nov
Ylir	Warmth	mid-Nov to mid-Dec

Hrutmanudhur	Ram Month	mid-Dec to mid-Jan
Thorri		mid-Jan to mid-Feb
Goa		mid-Feb to mid-Mar

There were two seasons recognized by Old Norse Custom: Summer and Winter. The year began with the first day of Summer, 1st of Harpa (Somerdag) and Winter began on the 1st of Ylir (Vinternal). In other words, Summer Day and Winter Night. These two terms are less of a technical translation, and more of a feeling. The idea of Day and Night was overriding, even in the yearly calendar.

In Iceland, the Thing took place four weeks after Summer started and no later than eight weeks before Vinternal. The Althing took place after ten weeks of Summer had passed.

Einmanudhur means "first month" and can be seen at the beginning or the end of the calendar. It's more of a 'gray time.' Although it is more logical to look at it as a part of Summer, rather than Winter, it was considered a Winter month and that is why it can be found at the end of most calendars instead of at the beginning.

One of the reasons that it is harder to place a specific correlation on the Old Norse Calendar is because some months were longer than others. The months could vary in length from 24 to 35 days. But they average out to about what is shown above. They, therefore, did not observe the Solstices and Equinoxes. The calendar had to be amended each year. Since these amendations were done locally, it was up to the kings to decide when to celebrate Jul.That decision would, therefore reset everyone's calendar for the coming year.

DAYS OF THE WEEK
It was no mistake that most of the days of the week are named what they are. Out of the seven days, four of them are dedicated to deities of the Aesir and the Vanir, and two more are named for the heavenly beings Sunna and Mani. Only one day's name comes from another culture, that being Saturday, named for Saturn. To the Norse, it was known as Laugardagr (Bath Day). The Vikings

74

were a very clean people, unlike much of the rest of Western Europe. It is quite possible that, because of the tradition of washing and cleansing, Scandinavia had fewer problems when The Plague spread over the European mainland.

Day of Week	Named For
Sunday	Sunna
Monday	Mani
Tuesday	Tyr
Wednesday	Odin
Thursday	Thor
Friday	Freyja
Saturday	Saturn

The times of the day were split up into, roughly three-hour segments. This was fairly standard, culturally, and was easily calculated by the movement of the sun or moon across the sky (for most of it).

Time of Day	Name of Time
6 am	Rismal/Midur Morgunn
9 am	Dagmal (Breakfast)
12 (noon)	Hedegi (Midday)
3 pm	Undorn/non (Mid-afternoon)
6 pm	Midur aftann (Mid-evening)
9 pm	Nattmal (Night meal)
12 (midnight)	Elding/Otta

SACRED WEAPONS

Many Pagan traditions ask whether an item is a tool or a weapon. It sounds like a fairly easy question to answer but there is a lot wrapped up in it, if you think about it. The first thing that comes to mind is the item in question; a sword, a knife, an axe, a staff, etc. Of course they're all weapons. But anything can be a weapon. Just ask your friendly neighborhood ninja. So the item can be a weapon, yes. In the Wiccan traditions, as well as some other Pagan paths, some of these are used as altar tool to represent something else (god and goddess, elements, etc). Therefore, they are tools. But I am not going to answer this question for you. That's up to you to answer it for yourself.

However, the second thing we must think about is consecration. If something is sacred, what makes it so? Now we have to start thinking about definitions again. So let me help you. We tend to bandy the words "Consecrate, Holy, Hallow, Sanctify, Sacred" about. In doing a study of these words, I found some very interesting information.

The word 'Holy' comes directly from the Old Norse by way of both German and Saxon. In German, the word is 'heilig' and in Saxon, 'halig.' The word 'Hallow' means the same thing: Associated with the gods, or, religious or morally pure. I refuse to bow to temptation and start a rant on 'morally pure.' We are supposed to be talking about Sacred Weapons.

The word 'Consecrate' comes from the same Latin word for 'Sacred' or, 'sacer.' This means to be devoted to a deity, regarded with deep and solemn respect; entitled to veneration or worship. It also means it is not to be challenged, violated or breached under any circumstances. In other words: holy. Sanctify means to make holy or declare legitimate or binding.

So, why is this important when talking about Sacred Weapons? Because there are three ways to consecrate something: By making it, by ritual, or by use in a holy manner. In any of the three cases, the now sacred object has a story behind it and the story is what feeds the respect and veneration of the item as holy. Which leads me back to Sacred Weapons. It's true, then, that any weapon, any tool, can be made sacred. That being said, I refuse to get into a discussion about respect of tradition. Just because something *can* be made holy, doesn't mean it *should*.

77

The Ancient Norse believed that only three weapons could be considered sacred, because of the direct connections they have to the gods. These were; the Spear, the Hammer and the Axe.

The Spear carries a long tradition. It is considered a symbol of authority and is connected to Odin. It was also the first weapon wielded in the first war between the Aesir and the Vanir. It was also traditional for the Norse warriors to follow Odin's example by throwing a spear over the heads of the enemy as the first act of battle.

The Hammer was originally made of stone (incidentally, 'hamar' is an Old Norse word for stone). But Thor's hammer, Mjollnir, is used, not only as a weapon of war, but also to bless blóts, cups, marriages, etc. Just because it is a sacred weapon does not mean it doesn't have more than one use.

The Battle Axe is more connected to the Vanir than the Aesir. During the first war, Njord used an axe to hew open the gates of Asgard. Don't get the impression that the axe is an offshoot of the hammer. They are two distinct weapons and are used differently in battle. They also have different magical uses.

Each of these weapons is associated with a different point on the compass: hammer in the North (because of Thor's wars with the Jotn, there), axe in the West (because Vanaheim is in the West of the Underworld) and spear in the East (due to the location of Asgard, but to explain that one would get me into all sorts of arguments with the experts).

There is some conjecture that the club should also be considered sacred. But the club is more connected to man than to the gods. If we include it, we should also include the stag horn, due to Frey's use of it at Ragnarok. And maybe, after Ragnarok, it too will be considered sacred.

The sword was not considered a sacred weapon until relatively recently. Originally, all swords were thought to be cursed and there are many accounts in the ancient writings of cursed swords. I can find no accounts of a cursed hammer or a cursed battle axe, however. During the Golden Age, a few of these swords had survived from more ancient times. Angantyr's sword, Tyrfing, could not be sheathed until it tasted blood. This sword was made by Volund, stolen by the gods, stolen from them by a long line of heroes and became the bane of every owner's existence. Such stories were typical of swords and therefore, all swords were originally thought to carry a curse upon them. This idea can also give us a little clue as to the date of an Eddic tale or Saga, too. If the story talks about a wonderful, blessed sword, it is most likely a later work...or, at least the version we are reading is.

The Bow was another weapon, which was not considered sacred, although it has a deep connection to Hod and Ull. The reason is that it was an arrow, which brought about the death of Baldur. But don't get me wrong. Although there were marvelous swordsmen and famous archers among the gods and their allies, some weapons could be considered sacred and others could not.

The knife, in its various forms, was not considered a sacred weapon, either. This was a tool that was used, not only as a weapon, but also in everyday life. It was a mundane tool with no sacred connection. This doesn't mean that it cannot be blessed, or consecrated, however. Anything can be consecrated for a specific purpose. I am speaking of weapons with a historical/mythological basis for consecration.

WHAT IS RITUAL?

Before we discuss Norse Ritual, we need to lay a little groundwork. So, let's start by talking about what ritual is.

Ritual is anything we do the same way (or variants of that way) on a regular basis. This can be something we do daily or something we only do once a year (or, for that matter, once in our lives). But we still do it the same way. Sometimes, those rituals are a game we play. Other times, they're deadly serious. But, we are ritualistic creatures by nature. Ritual helps us define and recognize our place in the Universe. It helps us strengthen, or establish our bond with self, deity, and other people or beings. Some rituals are personal. Some are religious and some are cultural, such as Rites of Passage.

So....what is the difference between ritual, habit and superstition? Habit is an act with little to no thought behind it. It is something that is done for, at best, immediate gratification and nothing more. Superstition is an act with an element of fear at its foundational level. It is an act, which has no logical connection to its expected outcome. And, it is a process by which we allay that fear. (Example: "See a pin, pick it up. All the day you'll have good luck," carries the implication that I will not have good luck, if I do not pick up that pin.) Ritual, on the other hand, is something we do consciously, with will and intent.

All three; ritual, habit and superstition, can be taught, or they can be behaviors we build from our own experience. The problem arises when our superstitions bear the expected fruit. (Example: When I was a kid, we had a superstition in my family – we called it a tradition—that you must never wear a white shirt to the dinner table, if we were having spaghetti. Whoever did was sure to spill). Ask some people why they go to church on Sunday morning and you might get the response, "Oh my family's always gone here" or, "because it's the right thing to do." This has become habit. Ask someone why they cast flowers on the river and you might get the response, "to honor the Earth and to show my love and respect for it." This has become ritual.

Sacred Ritual – both public and private – is a way to express our will and intent before the gods. It also gets us into a proper frame of mind to be in their presence.

NORSE RITUAL

There are three elements: Ice; represented in the North, Water; represented in the South, and Creative Wisdom; represented in the Center. These are the elements by which everything came into being. The three small cups hold water; Ice cold saltwater in the North, Hot earthy-tasting water in the South and tepid water with a little honey added in the Center cup. The horn should be filled with only enough mead that the water(s) can be added to it.

Any setting of ritual space is done by way of embracing the Creation Myth, where Odin and his brothers killed Ymir and made Midgard through the use of his bones, body, and blood. On the physical plane, the ritual space is set apart by three Hazel rods, placed in the corners. The area takes its shape, direction and Hazel posts from the old temple design and practices. Hazel is the wood of judgment and announces the area as sacred (this is due to its association with Baldur).

The gods are called upon singularly, or in any combination necessary, depending on the work to be done. In many instances, no deity is called... It is assumed S/He is there. It is also accomplished by more of a meditation than an invocation or evocation.

The Deities and Elements are not dismissed. This is because the gods and elements of life and creation are always present, no matter where we are. A simple, "This rite is finished," will suffice.

The altar is set in this way:

North	Center	South
Cup	Cup	Cup

Horn

Personal
Tools

Please note that the shape resembles the Mjollnir.

Personal tools would consist of any personal tool that represents your connection to the deities being called *or* whatever materials being used for the working: Runes, Herbs, your sacrifice or offering, etc.

NOTE: *Unless it is specifically called for, no knives or weapons are allowed in the altar room during ritual. This is especially true of any workings with Frey, as Frey gave his sword as a betrothal gift and is killed by it at Ragnarok.*

The ritual shall start this way:

Make the Sign of Mjollnir over North cup
Face North and say:
From Hvergelmir and the Svarkaldr Saer comes the icy rime-mist: The Endurance of Man

Make the Sign of Mjollnir over South cup
Face South and say:
The icy mist mixed with the warmth that rose from Urd's Well: The Jardr Magn. Earth's Strength

Make the Sign of Mjollnir over Center cup
Face Center and say:
Above Ginnungagap, the icy cold and the warmth contended with each other until they were mixed with the Sonar Dreyri of Mim's Well. Wisdom and Creativity bound them together

Make the Sign of Mjollnir over Horn and pour the mixture into it
Face Altar and say:
Mixed with Mead, we drink to the gods for peace, power, loyalty and friendship.
Drink and refill the horn with Mead

Odin set the Four Dwarves to hold Ymir's skull, the vault of heaven. Ostri, Sudri, Vestri, Nordri, your work is acknowledged.

We cross Bifrost to Asgard, to commune with the gods. We stand at the gates as Gylfi did; to give and receive in return.

Here, if specific deities are called, a short meditative prayer may be spoken. This is also the time to say something about the particular Blót, Sumbl or working.

Pick up the horn and make the NAUTH rune over it three times, intoning it as you do.

ᚾ   ᚾ   ᚾ

I sing as Ale-Runes, and bless the horn with the sign of Mjollnir
Here is where the Order of Horns is drunk. Or, at a Sumbl, it can be included in the feast.
At the Blóts, here is where the Rites of the Sonar-Golt and the Braggarkup would be performed.

Drink the whole horn

Here, the working is accomplished or you repair to the room where the Feast is held

The offering is blessed and given to the gods for a successful working

GALDR AND SEIDH

There is so much talk, nowadays, about two traditions in Norse Magic: Galdr and Seidh, that it is important address this topic. Galdr is an Old Norse word that is translated as 'magic.' It involves the use of runes and chanting. Descriptions of Galdr can be found in many sagas and Eddic poems and I would encourage the reader to pay special attention to Havamal vs. 146-164, known as the "Rune Poem" Grogaldr vs 5-15, and Sigrdrifumal vs 6-22. (Also, please see the section on Poetic and Musical Styles) These are all examples of Galdrwork as secret incantations or spells sung for a specific purpose. Except in a couple of cases, they are not the runes of the Elder Futhark. Where people get confused is the use of the word, 'rune.' But, we already know that 'rune' means 'secret,' as well (see section on Runes). Galdrwork is not ceremonial. In no place that I can find, is any ceremony suggested for Galdrwork. In fact, there seem to be accounts describing Seidhwork as having more ritual connected to it, than Galdr. Those additional ritual aspects, by the way, included Galdrsongs on many occasions.

Galdr is a tradition involving magical song or incatation (see above references). It is not a tradition using the runes of the Elder Futhark. The word 'rune' in these passages means 'secret incantaion.' I can find no place where Odin gave Galdr to man, but man used Galdr in any number of the Sagas. I CAN find where the runes of the Futhark were given to man, but not Galdr. This does not mean that we cannot use songs to effect magic. We know from experience that we can, and do. In Chapter 3 of Germania, Tacitus records an account from an eye witness, who clearly saw the Eleventh Galdrsong in action, as described in Havamal 156.

Ynglingasaga is very clear in connecting Seidh to Freyja. In the Old Norse, Chapter 4 says; *Freyja kendi first medh Asum seidh.* "Freyja first taught Seidh to the Aesir."

Seidh work is a very complex discipline, but at the same time, it seems to be rather flexible. It may be able to incorporate practices from other magical cultures, making it very eclectic. Some call it Norse Shamanism, but I would be very careful about using that word.

I knew a woman who claimed to be a third generation shaman. One July, we had a devastating rainstorm, which flooded my house. I don't mean two inches of water in the basement, I mean the rain broke through my roof, soaking the bedrooms on the second floor, ran through the walls and ceiling, ruined my kitchen, living room and dining room and then into the basement. Lights were filled with water. We couldn't use the electricity in certain rooms for a few days, while the wires dried out. It was the most devastating rainstorm I had ever experienced. The next day, I got a phone call from this woman, who said, "How'd you like that little storm I cooked up last night?" I nearly sent her the bill for the new roof.

I don't know if this person truly caused that storm. But she was willing to take responsibility for it (hm, there's another lesson there, somewhere). She obviously didn't understand what a devastating effect such a storm would have on the people who live around her. If memory serves me, no one died in the storm, but people's homes were destroyed. If she did cause it, she was splodging energy all over the place and it was out of control. It had much the same effect as giving a toddler a machine gun and teaching him how to pull the trigger.

Many people hold the belief that 'Seidh,' like the English word 'seethe,' means to boil over with emotion. They think that Seidh work is a lot of writhing around and frothing at the mouth, totally out of control. They spend a lot of energy till they are completely physically drained, and call it Seidh. But this is not the case. The two words are not related. 'Seethe' comes from the Old Norse word 'soudhr,' which means to boil meat. The word Seidh has no single English counterpart and has never changed. It may be more closely related to the Sanskrit word, 'siddi,' meaning "work of power." Seidh is most often translated as magic or sorcery.

Etymologically, the word cannot be traced back to its roots, with any verifiable proof. However, equivalents can be found in Old High German and Old English to mean, 'snare, 'cord,' and 'string.' It is not connected to the Gaelic word that is even spelled the same way in English.

Seidhwork can involve trance work, charms and amulets, astral projection, but it also involves weaving, spinning, drawing and binding. It involves one's spiritual self, as much as one's physical self. It very often involves the employment of a drop spindle and making thread.

But at no time did it mean something just shy of a fit in a trancelike state. Remember, Seidh is a discipline, which requires a focused will and intent. This is very hard to achieve when one is completely out of control. The only thing that I can find about being physically drained after a magical experience is shape shifting. To be sure, Seidh can involve shape shifting, but so can other Norse magical paths, like Berserking. But it is not the Seidh that makes one over-tired. It is the shape shifting. Seidhworkers can be shape shifters but not all shape shifters are Seidhworkers.

All magic comes from the Jotn. Now that I have your attention, keep in mind that the gods are descended from the Jotn, much like the Greek gods were descended from the Titans. With the splits between the Jotn and the different pantheons of deities, certain magical gifts became associated with different groups. Shape shifting became associated with all groups, as did magical song. Astral projection became associated with Seidhwork, as did the use of wands, and amulets.

But to look for honor as a Seidhworker is a lost cause. Those who were Seidh workers were known as the witches. Though they were employed from time to time, they were often shunned, hunted, killed or banished from the land. The use of magic did not make you a witch. The Edda is very specific about how Odin used magic to put witches to flight. There are also suggestions about how to protect your home against witches.

Just because Seidh has, historically, been shunned does not remove it from being a viable practice. It is as necessary today as it was in Harald Fairhair's time. In many cases, the Seidh workers tended toward the darker practices. Laxdaela Saga chapter 49 tells then story of Gudrun spinning seidh to manipulate her husband into killing his friend. There are many accounts written in the Sagas where Seidhworkers were employed in times of war and strife. People also tended to seek them out to help them take revenge for one reason or another.

Physically, Seidhwork is done between the worlds. This could be done on a rooftop or raised platform called a Seidh tower. It doesn't necessarily mean that the higher you are, the more effective your work. But to be in a position off the ground is important. There is a particular energy, which you may feel while off the ground. It is a different energy than while standing on the Earth. This energy is important to Seidh.

RUNES

My editors have told me that I need to define a few terms, here. So, let's start with the word *Rune*. This is a word that has many meanings in Old Norse, depending on context. Where it may be translated as 'secret' in one place, it may mean 'message' in another. It can also mean 'mystery' and even 'meeting.' But the word was also used to specify a simple graphic design, which had cultural significance, or magical influence. This is the definition we will normally use in this section. But it is wise to keep the other meanings in the back of your mind, especially as they pertain to divination.

The Norse runes were used as a collection of magical symbols long before they were used as a way of writing. That use became more common with the development of the Younger Futhark, around 600 CE, that we are aware of. But archeologists are finding new things everyday and that last statement could change.

As you study the runes, you will find that, to our ancestors, the system was not absolute. There are variations in the Futhark, based on time period and location. It is important to point this out, since, with the current move toward standardizing a futhark, much insight can be lost in the shuffle. To say that the Futhark is absolute is quite like saying that the QWERTY keyboard is the only type of computer keyboard there is and that there is no other way to organize the letters of the alphabet onto it.

Incidentally, I'll bring up something here. The conventional names of the runes do not appear in any ancient language connected to the runes. They are reconstructed words to give them an older, more ancient sound and merely to standardize them. This is one way that standardization has become a trap.

I do not believe that standardizing a futhark is a bad idea, necessarily. But when we assume that that standardization is absolute, we are in danger of disregarding knowledge and insight from our ancient predecessors. Why limit the power and flexibility of the runes?

Hold on, Brad. You just used the word 'Futhark.' What's this 'futhark, of which you speak? The futhark is so called because when read as a word, that is what the first 6 runes spell. It's the same philosophy behind the word, 'alphabet,' which comes from the names of the first two letters; alpha and beta.

The Runes of the Elder Futhark is split into 3 families called *aetts*, each containing 8 characters. The word *aett* is translated as family, clan, or kin. But it is a root word that also carries other contextual meanings, such as lineage, and compass direction. This may be a fairly recent development in organizing the runes (say, in the last 100 years). The word has nothing to do with the English word eight. I disagree with the practice of attempting to name each of these three *aetts* in some 'overall' way. Why, for instance, would there be a Birth Rune in an *aett* categorized as 'Destruction?' Or, for that matter, A Fertility Rune in an *aett* named for 'Justice?'

There are certain Runes that are named for particular deities and others that we associate with certain deities because of similarity in attribute or power. But categorizing the Runes can take many forms.

There are also writers who have assumed that, originally, there were no runes with curved lines and that this made it easier to write in rock or wood. I suggest that these writers have never worked in either rock or wood. Nor, have they ever looked at ancient rock carvings. There are carvings in stone from many ancient cultures, which use curved lines and circles. There are futharks that date back to the 4th Century and before, which use both curved and straight lines. Quite frankly, many who experiment with Runes today have no idea where they come from or that there were so many variations on their meanings, not to mention how they were scribed. Some Runes have double and triple meanings. Some of these will be discussed later in the book. Now that I've irritated anyone who might endorse this book, let's move on.

The system I use is based on an amalgamation of two Futharks that date from the 4th and 6th Century CE. These two Futharks are the Kylver Stone Runes from Gotland Sweden and the Bracteates of Vadstena, from Gaumpan Sweden. I should caution you, however, that there have been corrections made to update the Futhark and therefore make it easier to understand by those who use other systems.

Kylver Stone Runes (ca 400's CE)

ᚠᚾᚦᚨᚱᚲᚷᚹᚺᚾᛁᚼᛁᚲᛃᛣᛊᛏᛒᛖᛗᛚᛜᛞᛟ

92

Bracteates of Vadstena (ca 500's CE)

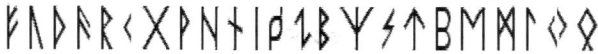

ᚠᚾᚦᚨᚱᚲᚷᚹᚺᚾᛁᛈᛇᛒᚢᛃᛏᛒᛗᚾᛚᛜ

Please notice that there are some differences between the two futharks and also differences from what is generally accepted as the Standard Futhark. Not only do the orders of the runes differ, but also the design and facing, in some cases. Of particular note, in the Vadstena Runes, is the use of ᛒ and ᛔ and the designs of ᛃ and ᛜ. In the Kylver Stone Runes, I was intrigued by the ᛜ, which looked very much like a backward ᚠ. Also, note the facing of the ᛒ. Additionally, I found it interesting that in both futharks, the size of ᚲ is much smaller, in relation to the other runes.

I do not subscribe to the philosophy that some Runes are inherently negative while others are wholly positive. This practice is shortsighted. To state that a Rune, coupled with another will always have only one meaning shows a lack of creativity. Our ancient predecessors may have had secret meanings for individual Runes, based on local tradition, but not two completely different sets of meanings based on purpose. Runes may have more than one meaning that may even seem contradictory to each other. Part of this is because the runes are dialectic. But the Runes will not have one set of meanings for magical purposes and another for divination. Since I've thoroughly confused you with that last statement and now have you in my power, we can continue.

In researching runic lore, one will find accounts as to the number of ways that many of the Runes were used; both in magic and divination. It is important to take these dialects into account when attempting to catalog their meanings.

As I have already stated, many Runes have more than one meaning. These meanings changed over time and distance. They also changed from subculture to subculture and can even have different meanings, depending on occupation. English is no different. For instance, if I am talking to a sailor and I use the word "tack," he will immediately think of sailing across the wind, turning, and sailing back across in a zig-zag pattern. If I mention that same word to an upholsterer, he will immediately think of the little nails used to hold fabric on to a chair. In today's English, the

93

term 'to let' means to allow. Three or four hundred years ago, it meant, 'to hinder.' If you ask someone for sugar in the north, you'll get a bowl full of white stuff to put in your coffee. Down south, you'll get kissed. I explained the difference to a friend of mine from Tennessee, once. All she said was, "Well, bless yer heart."

Before we get completely off topic:
Some of the Runes have a direct connection to particular deities – either by name or attribute. Other Runes have no such connection, except possibly by extrapolation. In the following pages, I've included a chart and a SHORT suggestion as to how each Rune can be used. Some of the meanings may seem contradictory to each other because many Runes can be used in more than one way. Longer descriptions of each are included in the next chapter.

THE ELDER FUTHARK

First Aett:

Rune	Ancient Name	Standard Name	Sound	Translation
ᚠ	Fe	Fehu	F	Property, Cattle, Prosperity
ᚢ	Ur	Uruz	U	Sleet, Drizzle, Sparks
ᚦ	Thurs	Thurisaz	TH	Active Defense, Protection
ᚨ	Os	Ansuz	O, A	God, Wisdom, Inspiration
ᚱ	Radh	Raido	R	Riding, Protection against Fire, Death Journey
ᚲ	Kaun	Kenaz	K	Sore, Boil, Blister
ᚷ	Gyf	Gyfu	G	Magic, Protection against Curses
ᚹ	Wyn	Wunjo	W	Glory, Achievement

Second Aett:

Rune	Ancient Name	Standard Name	Sound	Translation
ᚺ	Hagl	Hagalaz	H	Hail, Destruction, Natural brute forces
ᚾ	Nauth	Nauthiz	N	Need
ᛁ	Is	Isa	I	Ice
ᛃ	Ar	Jera	J	Year, Harvest, Sharing Good Fortune
ᛇ	Eoh	Eiwaz	EI	Strength, Flexibility, Yew Tree
ᛈ	Pertho	Peord	P	Birth, initiation
ᛉ	Eolh	Algiz	Z	Active Protection
ᛋ	Sigl	Sowelu	S	Sailing, Sun, Lightning, Speed

Third Aett:

Rune	Ancient Name	Standard Name	Sound	Translation
ᛏ	Tyr	Tiwaz	T	Justice, Equity
ᛒ	Bjarkan	Berkana	B	Love, Healing, Birch
ᛖ	Eh	Ehwaz	E	Confidence, Leadership, Morale
ᛗ	Madr	Manaz	M	Man, Servant Henchman
ᛚ	Logr	Laguz	L	Prosperity, Cleansing, Travel, Power
ᛜ	Ing	Inguz	NG	Fertility, Conception
ᛞ	Daeg	Dagaz	D	Day, Revealing
ᛟ	Othil	Othila	O	Clan, Ancestors, Legacy

ORGANIZING THE RUNES

Aside from the traditional way of organizing the runes in the three *aettyr*, there are other ways that could be taken into consideration:

By name of a specific Norse Deity

ᚦ	THOR
ᚠ	ODIN
X	GYF
ᚱ	HOENIR
↑	TYR
◇	FREY

Only one names a specific animal

ᚠ	Cattle

Times are self-explanatory

᚜	Year
ᛗ	Day

Tangible, elemental forces

<	**Fire**
ᚾ	Sleet
ᚺ	Hail
I	Ice
⚡	Lightning and Sun
ᚱ	Water

MEANINGS OF THE RUNES

Some of the information you find here may be startling, at first. We, as humans, have a tendency to accept what has been written previously without doing our own research. Consequently, I find that much of what is written about Runes to be broad generalization, assumption, or lacking adequate foundation. I actively encourage you to study the books listed in the bibliography.

As I have already stated, many Runes have more than one meaning. The meanings changed over time. A language is constantly evolving and meanings can change dramatically over long periods of time. The language of Old Norse was no different and neither are the Runes. If you read the chapter on Synthesis, you will understand what I am saying. The same rules apply to interpreting the Runes and what has become generally accepted in recent times.

The more I study the Runes, the more things change. I find that the ancient Rune Poems bear little resemblance to generally accepted interpretations and meanings. But this does not, necessarily mean that the generally accepted meanings are false. It only means that the more I learn, the more my understanding of the Runes deepens.

Another reason there can be more than one meaning has to do with cultural emphasis. What was important to the peoples in the Southern Germanys may have carried less importance to the Sviar or the Goths, farther North. To assume that the Runes were standard and unchangeable over hundreds of years of use and thousands of miles is to sell them short.

ᚠ

FE/ FEHU

Cattle, Prosperity, Wealth, Property Sheep, Livestock.

In ancient times owning cattle or sheep was an important way of measuring a man's wealth and standing in the community. So important, that it has its own Rune. This is tangible, measurable prosperity. By extrapolation, this is moveable wealth. But this is not to say that it cannot be used to attract intangible prosperity. It can be used in conjunction with other Runes to fully define that which you are working toward. The ancient Norse were peoples who worked hard for what they got and blessed the gods for it.

Magically, look for opportunities to acquire that which you are striving for.

Fe is the Old Norse word for Cattle, sheep or livestock. The prosperity it speaks of is of the land and is worked for. This is not a Rune of luck. It is a Rune of reward for hard work.

ᚢ

UR/URUZ

Sleet, Drizzle, Sparks, Expressive Will, Strength

Ur is an Old Norse word meaning sleet, drizzle or the sparks that fly while smelting metal. In either case, Ur is a very aggressive Rune. Ur strengthens the will and the mind. It brings clarity of thought, disregarding the 'fluff' and focusing on the desired result. Ur is considered by many to be masculine because of its aggressive nature.

Commonly called the Aurochs, only ONE generally accepted Rune Poem – The Anglo-Saxon Rune Poem – makes reference to this.

ᚦ

THURS/THURISAZ

Thor
Active Defense, Protection

This is the Rune of Thor. This is not a Rune of uncontrolled destruction. It is a Rune of protection, active and alive. It is a Rune of active defense. This is the War Hammer, not the Shield. This is the sound of Thunder, which is also associated with Thor.

Thurs is a Rune of aggressive activity. There is nothing passive about it. Thurs strikes in defense, but it is not a Rune of unmitigated attack. Thor is the protector of the gods. This means that he also protects their interests. Thor is also the protector of the common man. If using Thurs harms someone unnecessarily, it is HE you will have to deal with.

Thurs is a Rune of right vengeance. Use it carefully from the right motive.

ᚠ

OS/ANSUZ

Odin
Wisdom, Inspiration, Poetry, Deep Understanding (beyond knowledge), Leadership

Os is an Old Norse word for god and Odin's name comes from this word. His attributes are the attributes of the Rune and he can be accessed through this Rune.

Just as Odin is the god of kings, so Os is the Rune of kings and leadership. It is also most often understood to be the Rune of inspiration and wisdom.

As a Rune of poetry, it is also connected to Braggi, but that connection comes through Odin. Os has sometimes been viewed as a Rune of masculine virility. Though I can find nothing in the ancient writings about this, there is a certain sense to it, due to its connection to Odin.

ᚱ

RADH/RAIDHO

Riding, Protection against Fire, Death Journey

Radh has many meanings and uses. Radh is a 'Wave Rune.' This means that anything that moves in waves is affected by it. Hence, water, fire, herds, death, love, emotion, ships are all examples of things that move in waves. If Radh only meant 'riding a horse,' it never would have been placed in the longhouses as protection against Fire and Disease.

Radh can be connected to many deities. As a Death Rune, it is connected to Frygg, Baldur and Ran. As a protection against fire, it is connected to Thor, as he is the only god Loki truly fears.

The word Radh is East Norse and the same as Raidho. But in the East Norse, it has added connotations. It is also the sexual intimacy during betrothal and before marriage. Up until the early 1900's Rada (from ON Radh) still had this meaning in Swedish Provincial language. With such a connotation, it is also connected to Freyja and Gefjun.

ᚲ

KAUN/KENAZ

Sore, Boil, Ulcer, Blister

The Old Norse word for this rune is Kaun, not Ken, which has a completely different meaning that is only used in the Anglo-Saxon Rune Poem.

It can express anything from the need for physical healing to a minor irritation that impedes progress. Magically, it has been used effectively for everything from enlightenment to physical healing.

X

GYF/GEBO

Gyf

Gyf is a rune of 'deep magic from the dawn of time' (if I may coin a phrase). This is one of the few runes actually named for a deity. Gyf is the father of Nanna, the wife of Baldur and the leader of the Myrk-Riders, a very ancient tradition of magic users. Their existence predates the worship of the Aesir. In the old tales, the Myrk-Riders were also known as the Gyfir.

Gyf can also be used as a protection against curses. Only the Anglo-Saxon Rune Poem has an entry for Gyf and describes it as, "..furnishing help and assistance to all broken men who are devoid of aught else." Where so many assume this means 'a gift,' keep in mind that it is common for people only in very dire circumstances to finally cry out to a deity for help.

ᚹ

WYN/WUNJO

Hoenir

Glory, Achievement, Banner, Success

Wyn denotes glory or success. It is the Rune of achievement. As such, it is connected to Hoenir, Odin's brother, whose title, Ve, means banner.

A banner is raised to show success or glory. It is also the standard, which becomes the rallying point during battle or struggle. Rallying behind the banner brings strength to those in the thick of battle; not only morally but tangibly.

When casting the Runes and Wyn comes up; ask the Runes what the rallying point is. This will help you to find the path to the success suggested in the rune.

ᚺ

HAGL/HAGALAZ

Hail, Natural Destruction, Warning, Making way for the new

Natural destruction can come from any direction, not just ice pellets falling from the sky. Hagl can warn that things outside of your control may happen. But there is also an element of hope involved with Hagl. In many cases, destruction of the old must occur to make way for the new. This is not always the case, but may be dependent on other Runes in the reading.

If Hagl comes up in a reading, look for additional information. From which direction is the destruction coming from? Can it be guarded against? Is there an ultimate purpose behind that destruction?

To an ancient migrating people, or an agrarian culture, Hail was one of the worst things that could happen. Its force could devastate crops, harm beasts, goods and shelter. But if Hagl comes up, do not automatically think it is specifically directed at you alone. Hail falls on everyone. It is not selective.

ᚾ

NAUTH/NAUTHIZ

Need, Need-Fire, Magic, Fulfillment

Nauth is the Old Norse word for Need. This is something so basic to our existence that it cannot be denied, such as food, shelter and freedom from pain. When Nauth shows up in a Rune reading, take special heed. Something so foundational to the question must be fulfilled.

There was an ancient custom of making a large fire to carry prayers to the gods. This was known as the Need-Fire. Nauth is something far more foundational than want.

Nauth is a Rune of direct magic, seeking a solution to a question or problem.

I

IS/ISA

Flow-stopper, Barrier, Slow Progress. Also Temporal Beauty, Allure, Treachery

Think of all the things you know about Ice. This is Is. Is can stop things from happening, including travel. It can become a wall that is virtually impassable, slowing or even stopping progress. But Is is also beautiful. The colors and crystalline structure trapped within can be fascinating and alluring. Is is not the soft and delicate beauty of a Spring flower. It is the hard beauty, ever changing in the sunlight. It may appear fragile but it can re-form from day to day, showing its creativity. Ice, formed over water, can be treacherous. What may look safe can crack and break without warning, sending enemies below an impenetrable ceiling. It can shatter boats, form land and expand to break its bonds.

Is can be used to halt a direct magical attack. It has also been successfully used to trap malignant spirits so they can be removed and gotten rid of.

AR/JERA

Cycle, Harvest, Year, Sharing Good Fortune

Many ancient deities have a connection to Ar, including Frygg, Frey, Ostara, Sif and Idun.

Ar speaks of that which now comes to fruition. What is ready to be reaped has been growing within its cycle and now becomes full.

Ar can speak of what is ready, but it can also give hope for the future. It can give a time frame to watch or an event to look forward to.

Just as there is a clear definition between the sides of the Rune, and there can be a clear definition between the two halves of the year, a clear definition between early and late progress in a matter can also, sometimes, be seen.

An important concept to keep in mind; the 'plenty' that is harvested; it is to be shared with the community. This is alluded to in the rune poems.

109

EOH/EIWAZ

Strength, Flexibility, Yew tree

Eoh is a word with many inferences. First, it means Yew, a wood sacred to the gods. Before the Aesir built Asgard they lived in the Yew Dales, (the home of Ull). It was a time of peace and tranquility between the creation of Midgard and the first war. Because of the yew's qualities (lightweight, strong and flexible) the best bows were made from it. Hence, Eoh is known as the Archer's Rune.

Its mythology is as diverse as its history. In the OIRP it is 'bent bow and brittle iron.' In the ASRP it is 'reliable equipment for a journey.' Cynewulf used the Rune to mean 'wretched.' But the NRP says:

> *Yew is the greenest of trees in Winter*
> *It is wont to crackle as it burns*

I have often wondered if this was not a kenning for healing on the battlefield.

Here is an anomaly. The ASRP calls this rune Eoh. The OIRP calls it Yr. Yet, in the ASRP, Yr is not the yew. It is the name of one of Fraya's Shield Maidens. Yr is an Old Norse word for Bronze or Copper. This is also rune of physical wealth.

Yr is a source of joy and honour to every prince and knight;
it looks well on a horse and is a reliable equipment for a
journey.

ᚲ

PERTHO/PEORD

Birth, Initiation

Pertho is probably the most misunderstood Rune in the Elder Futhark. It has been called the Unknown, or Random Rune, The Dice Box, The Table Game, the Birth Rune and the Apple. A case can be made for all of these interpretations.

As a Birth Rune, it is not the Rune that protects the mother at birth. It is the Rune that protects the baby. Pertho is Initiation. It speaks to dramatic change – inside and out; where you are and who you are. It brings one through the initiatory experience, but gives no understanding or sense of hope. Because of this, it can leave one in a state of confusion.

But it can also be interpreted as 'a flute made of Pear Wood,' which makes more sense in light of the Anglo-Saxon Rune Poem, the only rune poem it shows up in. The rune's first use, however, can be traced back to the Kylver Runes of the 400's.

ᛉ

EOLH/ALGIZ

Active Protection, Hiding, Elk

Eolh is an active protection in battle, whether it's verbal or physical. It is not the shield, but rather, that which turns aside the weapons waged against us.

But Eolh is also the root word for Elk. As a large beast, it can still hide, unseen in tall grass; its antlers blending in with the landscape. In other words, hiding in plain sight. This becomes a very useful Rune for placing one's self in a position for any covert activity. Used in conjunction with other Runes, it has the ability to 'blend in' with them, thus, rendering magical processes undetected until the proper time.

There is much confusion about this one in the Runic Community. Don't sell it short and don't take it for granted. It has more than one use, covert and overt. Each of the ancient Rune Poems concentrated on one of its uses. None of them explains them all.

ϟ

SIGL/SOWELO

Sailing, Sun, Lightning, Quick Progress, Revelation

Here is where I defer to the ASRP. Most writers will tell you that this is a variation of the Sun wheel (or swatstika) and even use the other rune poems as proof. Keep in mind, however, that the name of that rune in the other rune poems is a LATIN word, not Old Norse, in origin. The Anglo-Saxon word for this rune is Sigel, which means 'to sail.' The ASRP makes it clear that this rune is about prosperity and safety while traveling by water.

Still, there is a conventional wisdom in having a rune for the sun or lightning and its effects. I have used it effectively, both ways, depending on how I was inspired.

Sowelo is the Rune of the Sun and Lightning. Things happen quickly, when Sowelo is used. The Sun can warm and promote growth, but it can also burn. Lightning can burn crops or start a fire. When Lightning strikes a tree, the tree may split. The whole area can be highly charged with energy. But the charge dissipates and the tree remains.Sowelo can charge something with vast amounts of energy very quickly. The down side is that "quick" does not always mean "permanent."

113

↑

TYR/TIWAZ

Tew

Justice, Balance, Equity, Decision, Judgment, Protection, Blessing, Self-Sacrifice (for the honor of the larger purpose), Nobility.

It has been speculated that, in very ancient times, Tew was the chief god of all. This assumption has also led to the assumption that his Rune is the Spear. It is also true that there were ancient tribes, cults and villages dedicated to the worship of Tew. But every tribe, cult or village had its patron or matron deity. Moreover, if this were the Spear, as many suggest, it would be the Rune of Odin, not Tew. Odin, who is known for his spear, is the chief of all the Aesir.

This is not the sign of the Spear, but of the Scale, complete with balance point. Tew is a god of justice and judgment. The Rune was scratched on weapons or body to elicit Tew's judgment, favor and protection in battle. This is also the Rune of Self-Sacrifice for the good of a larger purpose.

BJARKAN/BERKANO

Healing, Ease of Labor, Protection, Cleansing, Love Beauty, Death

Named for the Birch, Bjarkan is one of only two Runes named for trees. It is also one of the most active and versatile Runes in the Elder Futhark.

Bjarkan has been used for healing (both physical and emotional), to ease pains during labor, for protection against curses and disease, and cleansing of self or a space of unwanted energies. The Birch Tree is also known as the Lady of the Wood and is named so because of its association with Freyja. Due to this association, it is also associated with Love, Beauty and Death. Bjarkan is Feminine Nobility.

Birch has been seen as a versatile and powerful tree for so many thousands of years and in so many cultures, it is no wonder it has its own Rune. Magically, you'll find it very easy to work with and very forgiving.

ᛖ

EH/EHWAZ

Confidence, Leadership, Morale

I am often bemused by the fact that we call this Rune Eo, (which is based on the GREEK word for Horse) and not Jor or hross, the poetic and common words for horse, respectively. To assume that the Rune means Horse leads me to one conclusion: those who have written about this rune can't get past the first two words.

Troops take their sense of confidence from their leader. Without that sense of confidence, they get restless, nervous and fearful. The ASRP says,

> *The horse is a joy to princes in the presence of warriors.*
> *A steed in the pride of its hoofs,*
> *when rich men on horseback bandy words about it;*
> *and it is ever a source of comfort to the restless.*

This is the leader, bringing up the morale of his troops, before battle. He expresses his confidence in them and to them.

116

ᛗ

MADR/MANNAZ

Man, Husband, Henchman, Servant

This is simply 'Man' in all his aspects of being a man: his joy, his pride, his success. It also denotes man's sense of self and independence. This is also the husband, in the sense of being coupled with a mate; NOT in the sense of tending livestock or tilling the earth (there were other words for these).

But the word was also used in Old Norse to mean one's compatriot or one's trusted servant. These two meanings will depend on what Madr may be coupled with.

117

ᛚ

LOGR/LAGUZ

Prosperity, Travel, Power, Division, Cleansing

Water, is a source of prosperity. Fishing was an important part of the Norse culture. Fishing not only meant food, but prosperity and trade. Secondly, large bodies of water could be traveled to places for raiding and trading. Prosperity meant success in these endeavors, as goods and profit could be brought home again. Thirdly, deep water was seen as a place where one might find hidden treasure, such as the Nibelung Treasure.

Water is a strong and powerful natural force. Bodies of water were natural dividers between cultures. Water is a means of conveyance at any change in the life process. As such, it is associated with both the death and birth journeys.

Logr is an Old Norse word, which means to bathe. And cleansing was as important a concept to the ancients as the idea of large bodies of moving water. Water is also seen as the divisions between the nine worlds.

ING/INGUZ

Frey

Fertility, Conception, Seed, Start of Growth, Initiation

Frey, also called Ing, is the god of Fertility. This is one of the few Runes actually named for a deity. Ing is the Rune of Fertility in all its forms and attributes. It is the Great Initiator. As a Birth Rune it starts the whole process, taking potential and starting it on the road to reality. Ing is the beginning of bringing something into existence.

In Norse Mythology, the creation myth is founded on the idea that something already existed but was changed into a new thing. Rune magic can work the same way. But Ing almost defies this idea by suggesting that something can be crated from nothing: from possibility to reality.

119

ᛞ

DAEG/DAGAZ

Day, Revelation, New Circumstances

Daeg is Old Norse for Day, differentiating it from Night. This is the time between sunrise and sunset. But, extrapolating from that, it can also mean the time from sunrise to sunrise.

Just as each day is new, so we are new within each day. This carries with it the suggestion that what occurred yesterday is of less concern than what is occurring today. This is also the shining time, when things are revealed, just as we can see more in the sunlight. Look for revelation and understanding.

There is a balance between Day and Night, just as there is a balance between the Sun and the Moon. But as far as gender goes, Day, which is masculine, balances out the Sun, which is feminine. Night, which is feminine, balances the Moon, which is masculine.

120

OTHIL/OTHILA

Clan, Ancestry, Legacy, Allegiance, Authority

Though Othil is usually seen as the temporal family, it is much deeper than that. It is our history, our lineage and our allegiance to family through that unbroken line of ancestors. It is the authority of the bloodline. Othil can also mean that which comes to us by way of inheritance. In other words it is based on who we are, not what we do. We have little control over what we inherit from our ancestors. It is not something we can strive for, or attain to. It is us, because we are them. It is not a gift we can ask for, although we can ask to be taught about what has come down to us. Consequently, gifts, abilities, authorities become ours to inherit.

Othil is what we come by honestly, through no cause of our own. We can also use it in Rune magic to commit ourselves to an extended group, such as a Coven or Gard. But even here, we would not express such a commitment if it didn't already exist. Such is the way of true friendship and trust.

RUNE CASTING

The proper frame of mind and heart is very important. I suggest starting with a prayer, acknowledging Odin, who mastered the Runes as well as the Norns, who created them.

There are many ways to cast Runes for divination. The important thing to remember is what the positions mean when the Runes are cast. Knowing this will give you the context you need for interpreting them. In previous chapters, I have mentioned the importance of context. Rune reading is a perfect example of why.

Let us take the question, "Where is my love-life headed?" By the way, I made up this question as well as the casting while sitting in a roomful of people. This was not an actual casting I did for myself or anyone else. I only add it in here to prove a point about context. I pull three Runes: I ↑ ᛗ and position them; Past, Present and Future.

The I in the Past denotes conflict and the need for flexibility. As the Past leads into the Present, that conflict, though, has helped to define my dreams (↑ in the Present position) and what I truly need in my love life. ᛗ in the Future position denotes the promise of a coupling – the positive answer to the underlying question, "Will my love-life be happy?"(understood by the original question). The connection between the Present and the Future, ↑ and ᛗ would tend to say, "Follow your dreams. Listen to your heart." The reading either says this or that my next Significant Other will be a Bisexual Union Longshoreman. Sometimes the Runes can be tricky.

But what would happen if we looked at the positions differently? Keeping the same casting, but laying them in the positions; Background (of question), Challenge or Quest, and Outcome, we get a slightly different response. As Background of the question, I would indicate that I tend to be fighting myself in love and may need inner healing. It would beg the question, "Do I lean toward self-sabotage?" That being the case, it may give us clues about ↑ in the next position; 'What am I afraid of?' would be the indicated follow up question. The Runes seem to reveal that there is an emotional darkness that I may have to face and overcome to achieve success. ᛗ in the final position indicates the promise, based on successfully meeting that Challenge.

The positions give us a context in which to read and understand the Runes. Knowing the positions would mean knowing what the Runes are saying. It's much like the English language. If I write the word "wind" by itself, it means nothing. In fact, you may have a different image in your mind than the person sitting next to you. But what happens when I give the word a context?

There's a lot of wind, today.
He's nothing but a big bag of wind.
Let's wind this up.

Three different sentences, all using "wind" as the key word, with three completely different meanings because the context has changed.

Many books about Rune casting only give you one context. They will say, "This is how you read Runes." The first Rune will always mean _____ and the second Rune will always mean _____ (and so forth). The Gods have shown me this." Though books of this nature may be good in the beginning, they become self-limiting. The spreads are not bad in and of themselves. What becomes self-limiting is the idea that there is only one way to cast the Runes. With only one context, there can only be one way of reading the Runes.

But your abilities to read Runes come from your relationship to the gods and the Runes: not someone else's. Listen to your heart. What are the deities trying to tell you in context? You should know the contextual positions before you cast the Runes. Let the gods guide you.

Keep your Rune spreads simple. In most cases (though not all) the more detail you have, the more confusing the reading might become.

SINGLE RUNE SPREAD
The context here is the question itself, asking for a simple, direct answer in one Rune.

THREE RUNE SPREAD
There are many ways to use three Runes in a spread. The two most common are using the positions, "Past, Present and Future" and

"Root of the question, Path to follow (or Obstacle to overcome) and Outcome."

The Runes are picked out of the box, one by one and placed face down. Then each is revealed in turn and read. Look for connections between the Runes; just as one even in life leads to another.

CELTIC CROSS
The Celtic Cross is normally used in Tarot and there's nothing wrong with using it to cast the Runes. The key is still to understand the context of what you are reading. There are many variations of the Celtic Cross. The one you are most comfortable with is the one you should use. I only suggest that you keep this simple rule in mind: More Runes do not, necessarily, give you more information. In many cases, it only serves to confuse the reading.

RUNE CAST
Rune Casting is a more complex method of reading the Runes. While shaking them up in the box, ask the question at hand, and then pour out the Runes onto a cloth. The cloth represents the World, as we know it.

Any Runes that land face down are removed from the cloth and put away. This is also done with any that land on the edge of the cloth, as they have no immediate bearing on the question. The Runes which land face up should remain in the positions they landed.

Look for an overall pattern in the Runes, and then locate a start and a finish. This may be more difficult than it looks, sometimes, and takes practice. Once done, this spread will reveal a 'history' of the question from start to conclusion. It will include things to look out for and decision points to reach so that the conclusion shown will be attained. Pay special attention to Runes, which cover or touch other Runes. Also pay special attention to Runes, which point directly to others.

In some cases, two patterns may emerge, clearly indicated and separated by a space or chasm. Read each of these separately, as this can indicate that there is more than one force at work.

RUNE MAGIC

There are rules to effective magic, just as there are ways in which the natural universe works. Don't be fooled by someone who refuses to follow the order of things. Those who say they do magic and refuse to follow rules may get lucky once in a while. But, in my experience, they lack discipline. More often than not, their magic will fall flat.

There are also those who hide behind the term 'Shamanism' and say they don't have to follow rules. Such people insult true shamans by doing so. Shamanism is not an excuse for not following rules. The shaman merely accepts a different set of rules than most people may be familiar with. Shamanism is still a strict discipline. This is different than not following rules at all.

Rules apply to any magical process. But part of the problem is that the rules may look different from process to process. Rune magic is no different. Rune magic is more than carving graffiti into a dead tree or chanting funny sounding words by the campfire. It is as much a skill as it is an art.

In the Edda, the Sayings of the High One *(Havamal)* contains a section known as the Rune Poem. The steps for rune magic are clearly outlined in verse 144. These verses offer key words in a particular order for effective magical rune workings. These are the eight steps, given as rhetorical questions, from making to unmaking. They are asked as rhetorical questions; almost as a challenge, *Do you know how to...?"*

Viestu hve rista skal?
Viestu hve radha skal?
Viestu hve fa skal?
Viestu hve fiesta skal?
Viestu hve bidja skal?
Viestu hve blota skal?
Viestu hve senda skal?
Viestu hve soa skal?

Do you know how to cut them?
Do you know how to read them?
Do you know how to paint them?
Do you know how to test them?

127

Do you know how to <u>ask</u> them?
Do you know how to <u>sacrifice</u> them?
Do you know how to <u>send</u> them?
Do you know how to <u>destroy</u> them?

RISTA

I often marvel that cutting or writing the Runes is something that many people know how to do. When scribing the Runes for magical purposes, I do this in one motion, with the scribing tool never leaving the medium. This is to concentrate the continuous flow of energy, and connects it to the glyph. Proper mindset is very important in any magical process. If your mind is divided, you might find it more difficult to focus the energy as it is intended. But, I am not suggesting that over-concentration is better than no conscious concentration at all. One finds what works by experimentation.

RADHA

Radha is to read or consult. Comprehending the meanings behind the Runes is also very important. It is difficult to focus energy if you don't know what it is supposed to do. Learn the meanings of the Runes. Learn the foci of the Runes when coupled with other Runes.

A three-year old child may know the letters of the alphabet. Fewer know how to string them together to make meaningful words. This is no different than knowing how to write them *and* knowing how to read them.

Radha also means to consult. It is good to consult the Runes for direction when formulating the spell or process that is desired.

FA

Fa is to stain, color or paint. I have come in contact with some very elaborate theories about coloring Runes; different colors for different kinds of work, and so forth. There is little in the ancient writings to give us enough evidence of a general practice. We do know that the words stain and color were used in many ancient kennings to refer to blood, however.

I am not saying that using different colors for different kinds of work is wrong. In fact, if it works for you it is a practice that

128

should be continued. It all comes down to what triggers the proper magical response for you.

FEISTA

Means to test, prove, or understand. In any other discipline, one can test a theory or invention to see if it *will* work. The Norse were very practical people, remember. To build a test function into a magical process makes perfect sense. Doing so proves whether the magic will work the way it is intended. If the process does not work, change it. Whether the intent is correct becomes a question of ethics, not process.

So many times, in magic, there are adverse or no results. One of the reasons is because we truly do not know whether the process will work and we shoot blindly in the dark. Proving the effectiveness of the Rune magic eliminates this problem. There are various ways to prove or test the Rune spell.

1) Test it on a small or mild scale
2) Attempt the process in another area – away from the main intent
3) "Find the holes." Set the process into motion and look for the fallibilities. In other words, tear it down yourself.

Test before you start. There are fewer chances of things blowing up in your face.

BIDJA

This word means to ask, to supplicate or to pray for a thing. In following the steps we've outlined, it means to come before the gods knowing that the spell will work. This kind of confidence is very important to the magical process. The word is also translated 'to beg' or 'to wish.' I hesitate to use these meanings because in modern English, they tend to allude to a state of no confidence.

BLOTA

The verse following *Havamal* 144 says, "Aye, doth a gift look for gain." This philosophy is so basic to Norse Culture that it can be adapted to any dealings we have with the gods.

Anytime we deal in Rune magic we are entering the domain of the gods. When one enters another's domain, one gains permission to

129

enter out of respect. The Norse gods appreciate a strong will and a strong people. Being strong before the gods will gain their support more easily than being a sniveling weenie. But strong does NOT mean showing a lack of respect.

Another way to look at this verse is to say, "A gift demands a gift." The gods are allowing you entrance into their domain (magic). They are very willing to lend aid and support. A sacrifice to say thank you is very important. An offering or gift, such as food or something personal is a way of making sacrifice without killing horses or small animals. Please read that statement again.

SENDA

This is to set the magic in motion, sending it toward its intended goal. By now you know exactly what you are doing, have the proper means to get it done, have asked for and received the support of the deities and have said thank you...All before the working was accomplished.

To be honest, most people start at this step, may possibly say thank you and think they know what they are doing. According to this interpretation of the Havamal verse, their process lacks foundation. If they are lucky, something might happen. If they are truly unlucky, the gods could snuff them like a ten-cent candle.

SOA

This means to destroy or unmake and is just as important to the process as making is. When the working has been accomplished, pick up your tools. When you're finished playing, put your toys away. How many more metaphors can we use? By unmaking, or destroying the spell we send the energy back to where it came from.

Take a lesson from Thermodynamics. Energy changes but there is no more energy now, than when the worlds were created. Put it back when you're done using it. There are two reasons why the unmaking is important:

1) Protection. If the spell is unmade, it cannot be used against you. Granted, this depends on the working you are doing.
2) Energy changes. It evolves (or devolves, as the case may be). Too many people don't know how to put their toys

away. The residual energy may be fun for a while, but, like a small child unchecked, it can turn nasty if left to itself.

BIRTHRUNES

There are four Runes, which address the process of birth:

◇	Fertility or Conception
⟩	Gestation
ᛖ	Birth (to protect the baby)
ᛒ	Birth (to protect the mother)

Each Rune speaks to a different phase of the process. When two people are trying to become pregnant, ◇ will address this issue. It is the process of opening up the opportunities for fertility to become an active beginning. After conception is the period of gestation. Now, ⟩ comes into play. This is the growth, or, flourishing of that which has been conceived. During the actual birthing of the baby, two Runes protect the mother and the baby: ᛒ for the mother and ᛖ for the baby – thus, ensuring as healthy a birth as possible from both sides.

Other Runes can be used in conjunction with these:

ᚠ throughout the whole process.

ᛚ and ᚢ can be used in conjunction with ᛒ for the health and well being of the mother.

ᛚ, ᚠ and ᛒ are used in conjunction with ᛖ for the peace of the baby and ease of delivery.

133

RUNE STONES IN AMERICA

There has been some conjecture as to whether the Vikings ever made it to what is now North America. A small band settled on the East Coast, but only for a short time. Only a few credible stories handed down from the Native Americans have survived. These are important, because they corroborate the sagas of the exploring Vikings, stylized as they are. On the other hand, we have rune stones as far from the Eastern Coast as Oklahoma and Minnesota. These are not anomalies and they didn't spring up by themselves. In fact, many rune stones have been found.

Between at least 900 and 1400 CE the Viking explorers came to what they called Vinland and Markland and went West any number of times. In Heavener, Oklahoma there is a small number of rune stones that have been dated between 600 and 900 CE. But only 5 have survived.

I say 'survived,' because during the 1930's and 40's, collectors took many of the artifacts from that region and only about five (that we are aware of) have been preserved. The Kensington Runestone in Minnesota bears the date 1362 and was not discovered till the late 1800's. We know that King Magnus of Sweden sent an expedition to Greenland in 1355 that was never heard from again. It has been suggested that this artifact is from the same expedition party that Magnus sent out. We also know that Leif Eirickson and his family came to Vinland on more than one occasion to harvest timber for sale in Norway. With all this activity, I am even more intrigued that there is little archeological evidence of all these voyages. Could the Vikings have been so careful as to not leave any trace behind?

It has been suggested to me that rune stones found in North America were made in Norway and transported here. I was aghast, when I first heard this theory. It made no sense. Let's take the Kensington Runestone, for example. The reasoning goes like this: The stone is found in an area where no other formations of rock of its type could be found. Therefore, it must have been transported to the site it was found on. That type of grayish stone is very prevalent in Scandinavia and therefore it must have been transported from there. The Vikings must have brought it with them and placed it in its current location. If not the Vikings, then someone later – like a settler in the 1800's (when we had a large influx of immigrants from Scandinavia to Minnesota and the surrounding region).

Let's be practical, for a moment. The Kensington Runestone measures 36" x 16" x 6" and weighs well over 300 lbs. This weight is very important, as I am using it as the approximate weight of a very large man. The poor Scandinavians who migrated here in the 1800's were not about to risk their carts, horses and oxen on another 300 lbs that could do nothing for them in return. If it were some kind of family heirloom, Olaf Ohman, who discovered the stone on his property in Minnesota, would not have publicized it quite the way he did. Not to mention the fact, that, it never would have been taken from its original site in Sweden.

Now, let's talk about the translation. What is written on the Kensington Runestone is geographically specific (references to bodies of water, islands and length of journey). No one in Norway or Sweden could have been that specific without having knowledge of the area, or rather, without having been here to experience them.

Eight Goths and 22 Norwegians on a journey
from Vinland very far West.
We had camp by two rocky islands one day's journey North of this
stone. We were out fishing one day. After we came home we found
10 men red with blood
and dead. AVM save us from evil.

The side of the stone is inscribed, thusly:

Have 10 men by the sea to look after our ships 14 days' journey
from this island
Year 1362

There is another aspect to the Runestone's validity that no one, to my knowledge, has approached. That aspect is cultural. Runestones were produced for many reasons, including but not limited to: magical, religious, as physical boundary markers, to mark the site of a great deed or battle, or as a memorial to the dead. The Kensington Runestone falls under the last of these mentioned. Memorial stones might be raised at the burial site, but more often, they were raised where the person died. As such, it would have

136

been scandalous to move it. That act would carry as much import as moving a headstone in a cemetery, today.

The fact that no leader of the party is mentioned leads me to speculate three possible scenarios: a) that he died early in the journey or they separated from him, b) that there were current squabbles as to the true leadership of the party and discussion of mutiny might be in the air, or c) that the appointed leader had no previous fame, and therefore, no name. If he did something heroic, he would have had such honor.

The fact that not one of the dead is mentioned by name on the rune stone leads us to believe that their deaths were less than heroic. No one would have wanted an ignominious death to be written in stone and the story of the death is rather unspecific. It is written in such a way that a "kenning" could be construed from it.

Death by Tuberculosis, or another disease that might have caused a discharge of blood, would have been considered ignominious. But the disease could not be helped and there was nothing any member of the exploring party could have done about it. If the death were reported in an ambiguous way, anyone who read the stone later might be led to believe that they died in battle and the reputations of the dead were left in tact before the gods and men. Not naming them, then, became another face-saving measure. Honor was one of the most important things to the ancient Norse peoples.

The Heavener Stone in Oklahoma measures 12' x 10' x 16". It would have been more impossible for settlers, not to mention the traveling Vikings, to transport this massive rock, weighing tons, without a trace of the journey. The fact that it is so large and makes only one short statement: **ᚷᚱᛟᛗᛗᛖᛞᚨᛚ** makes this an important stone. Unlike the Kensington Runestone, the Heavener Stone is a boundary marker, clearly indicating the name of the Lord of the region.

(Glome's Dale or Glome's Valley).

The stone has been dated from between 600 and 900 CE, predating the Kensington Stone by at least 350 years. No other evidence of this expedition has been found. My theory is that the valley is named for him as a memorial.

137

In the same region as the Heavener Stone, is another, simply called the Poteau Mountain Runestone (La Flore County OK). It has been dated between the 7th and the 9th centuries and has a different inscription than the Heavener Stone. It reads: X⤒◇M ᚠ ᚱ ᚦ (please forgive me, the fonts that I have at my disposal are slightly different than the lettering used in the inscription).

$$X \dashv \aleph I M F \top D$$

The "experts" have disregarded it as 'not Viking,' for various reasons that make little sense. One used the logic that "it was too early for the Viking Period and therefore, not Viking." I'm not saying it was Viking, I say it's Norse. However, please keep in mind that; a) the Viking period is not the short span of time between 800 and 1100 CE. It lasted between roughly 300 and 1100 CE (please read the section on Migrations). Secondly, Viking "Dragon Ships" have been dated as early as 350 BCE (although, to be above board in my argument, all of those that were found are in Europe and Scandinavia). The early Norse had the means to travel this distance. Thirdly, if you can't read the inscription and don't know about mixing futharks, please don't call yourself an expert. Any high school-aged Swede can read this inscription, because they're still taught the Younger Futhark in school.

But, the way I read the Poteau Mountain Runestone inscription is different than what is commonly assumed.

For the most part, the characters are Elder Futhark, however the second character is clearly Swedish short-twig for 'a' (not 'l' as most assume). The third character, all the experts agree, is an '𐌗' or, a long 'O' sound. Finally, the last character is a 'ᚦ' not 'ᚠ,' as is commonly assumed. Consequently, they come up with a deciphering that reads Gloi(e)al(?).

The Poteau Mountain Runestone is not a word. It's a statement. Please look at the inscription again. The third character is '◇.' With the second rune being an 'a,' and the final rune being 'thurs,' it reads "GANGIEALTH."
It makes no sense until you separate the characters out this way;
GANG I E AL TH.

138

Now we turn to what we know about Runesters. They were not above using a sort of shorthand. This is an important concept in deciphering this text. The ᚦ at the end was commonly used to denote 'Tha,' which, in and of itself was the short form of the word, 'Thiggja,' meaning, 'to accept or receive.' The AL before it does not mean 'all' in the way it would if it were a prefix. In the middle or at the end of an Old Norse word, it was short for 'skulu;' 'shall, must or ought.' The first word, GANG is Old Norse for 'going' (it's where we get the English word). 'I' is 'to or toward.'

The only one I can't verify is ᛘ. Since we're looking at shorthand words in other parts of this inscription, my THEORY is that it is short for either 'EK,' meaning 'and' (same as 'OK') or that it is short for 'AKA,' meaning 'to drive, ' since 'ek' was also used as a variation of that word. Hence; "Going to drive and receive it all," or "Going to and ought to receive." In other words, "He's finally going to get his!"

If we turn our attention to Cultural Anthropology, there are two concepts I should mention that stand out here. The first is: Honor was very important to our ancient Norse predecessors. If a man had honor, he had a name. Nowhere in this translation is there a name. He could have been a bad leader, or he may not have won fame, yet. The point is there is no name. No name means no honor before the gods.

The other concept I want to bring up here is kind of interconnected with it. If this were a place that someone died in battle, a memorial stone would have been raised to him (providing he died with honor and was a respected leader). But he would not be buried under that stone. It would be there to commemorate where that man died. If the Poteau Mountain Runestone were a memorial stone, he certainly did not die with honor. The only way for him to save face in front of the gods would be if his name were not attached to that stone. Is this, then, a grave marker and a man is buried under that stone? I doubt it. I could be wrong, but I don't think so. If there is a man buried anywhere close to this stone, it would most likely be in an area that, at that time, would have been swamp or bog. He would have been given back to Erde.

At the risk of sounding contradictory, there is another possibility as to the reason why the Poteau Stone was made. It has been suggested that the reasoning behind it was magical. The stone

139

could very well have been scribed with runes to elicit the help of the gods in a war over land. Remember, that the Vikings who came here came from a long line of warriors, whose "prime directive" was to be the lords of all they surveyed. Could the Poteau Stone have been placed there with that intent? It's very possible, from a cultural sense, though not from an archeological sense.

There are scholars who believe that all of the stones in the Poteau Mountain area, including the Heavener Stones, were a 'runic puzzle' and all can be translated as dates corresponding to the Church Calendar. According to this theory, the Kensington Runestone was also included in this geographic puzzle, set in motion by Henricus, Bishop of Greenland. For this to be true, he would have had to command that the Stones in Oklahoma be raised 200 years before he was born and the Stone in Minnesota 150 years after he died. These dates are just approximates, mind you, but Henricus was installed as Bishop of Greenland in 1112 CE. Geologic testing has confirmed that the Stones in Oklahoma were raised between 600 and 900 CE and we know the date of the Kensington Stone. That's one powerful Bishop! It is more likely that the stones had nothing to do with each other and were not related in any way. Also, the Church was very much against teaching the runes as a method of communication. By papal edict, the Latin alphabet was to be taught and writing in any other cryptography became a punishable offense. To suggest that a Bishop sent Vikings out on a holy mission to raise rune stones would, most likely put his position in jeopardy with the pope. Henricus may well have come to Vinland on more than one occasion, but it is more than doubtful that he commissioned any rune stones to be raised in Oklahoma or Minnesota.

One of the reasons that scholars have trouble translating the runes is because a form of the Elder Futhark was generally used up until around 800 CE, when the Younger Futhark became more widely accepted (between ca. 800 and 1150 CE). Another reason they have trouble translating it is because the Futharks, themselves are very dialectic. Runes could change slightly or dramatically depending on where the runmaller, or scribe, was from.

Taking the translation of the Stone as stated above, "Going to and ought to receive," and looking at it through a warrior's eyes, it makes sense that the man referred to was dishonorable. Could this have been a spell to insure that the gods would investigate his dishonor and not hold his men to the same standard?

The Viking warriors were fond of placing spells such as this on their weaponry. A weapon may have a rune spell inscribed on it such as "Made by Thorval. This sword bites furiously," or "All this axe touches shall be vanquished." Such inscriptions are not uncommon among any ancient war-like cultures. If we look back at the Benjamite Slingers of ancient Israel we will find that they, too, inscribed their slinging stones with things like "Take that!" or "Ouch." The reasoning for inscribing weapons has a long history nearly everywhere in the world. The inscription, "Going to and ought to receive" on the Poteau Runestone has much the same feel to it. The problem with this possibility is that we have no archeological evidence to corroborate it. There is no evidence of a settlement of Vikings, nor, even, that they camped there enroute. There is no evidence that a battle ensued or children were raised in the area. All we have is the Stone, itself, and lots of speculation.

After all this, we still only know two things. The first is that Norse explorers did travel to this continent. Secondly, they left certain notes along the way; sort of like saying, "I was here", in petrological graffiti. How they got here and why they did not stay remains a mystery, which may never be solved. Nor, would anyone completely agree if it were.

VIKINGS IN AMERICA

It's amazing what can happen if we allow for mistakes. Throughout history, so many discoveries and inventions have occurred because of some silly mistake or another. The discovery of the Western Hemisphere by European explorers was no exception.

In the year 985 CE, Eirek the Red left Iceland to explore Greenland, hoping to settle there and build a new community. These were people who believed in the old ways and wanted nothing to do with this new religion called Christianity that was sweeping Norway and Iceland. Though Leif, son of Eirek had embraced this new religion, his father had not. Eirek set out for Greenland with his daughter, Gudrid and about thirty followers, one of whom was Herjolf, son of Bard, another Norwegian. Along the way roughly half the party died, primarily of sickness, and the rest made it to Greenland; Herjolf, being one of them.

Herjolf had a son, Bjarni, who was still in Iceland. Bjarni was a merchant and had decided to visit Herjolf and winter with him, as was their custom. He took his ship, manned with a small crew and sailed for the settlement in the Southwest of Greenland. Strong winds blew and storms turned the boat in other directions. What should have been a three-day journey took closer to seven, before the crew sighted land.

Bjarni allowed as how he didn't think this was Greenland and ordered his crew to continue sailing north, not allowing them to land. For 5 more days, they sailed, not finding Greenland, as they'd hoped. Finally,

Bjarni allowed the crew to turn the ship around and take advantage of the wind, which led them back to open sea. Four days later they landed in Greenland, very near to his father's farm.

It was fifteen years before he recounted his voyage for Eirek the Red and his sons, Leif, Thorvald and Thorstien. Leif decided to take a ship and see what these new lands were all about. He is considered the first to land in Vinland (roughly Nova Scotia) in the year 1000 CE and also to explore the lands of Markland and Heluland, so named by Bjarni. The whole area we are talking about is on the East Coast, between Baffin Island and Nova Scotia. It is possible that, at a later time, the Vikings traveled as far south

143

as New Jersey, but those are not the areas that they named Heluland, Markland and Vinland.

The sons and daughters of Eirek the Red came to this continent for one purpose: to harvest timber and bring it back to Iceland and Norway to sell. They did not settle the land for any length of time and found the Native Americans hostile to them. Leif did build houses, though, and lent them to his friend Thorfinn Karlsefni. Karlsefni intended to settle here with his wife, Gudrid, Leif's sister, sixty men and five women. Karlsefni traded and fought with the Native Americans and, in the end, returned to Greenland. This happened around 1010.

Because Eireksaga is a family account, we have more information about his children's experiences than other peoples. But the Eireksons were not the only Norse to explore this continent. There is evidence that the Norsemen explored as far west as Oklahoma and as far south as Texas, Louisiana and the Gulf of Mexico.
There have been rune stones found, which may be as old as the 600's CE and as recent as the 1300's. All of them are older than Cristoforo Columbo's "famous voyage" in 1492. Sagas like Eirek the Red's Saga may be stylized and slanted, but no more than Columbus'.

After the Karlsefni expeditions, there was little contact between the Western Hemisphere and the Nordic peoples. Just as in Greenland, the Vikings and their descendents were too intolerant of any native peoples, which did not espouse their own way of life. The whole idea was forgotten and became the stuff of fable and family saga.

144

HERBS – ABC'S

Herbs may be used for physical and emotional healing, and they may also be used magically. The ancestors also considered herb lore magical. What we will be discussing first, is the more magical uses, although there will be crossover from time to time.

There are seven herbs, which I will discuss briefly, rather than of a whole lot of them. This gives you the opportunity to study more in-depth, if you so desire. It is better that you knew a few very well, than so many that you lose the knowledge and forget them. If you need more than this list provides, there are any number of books on herbalism that can help. I like to keep things simple. Sometimes. On the other hand, I am quite amused by the many that speak with great authority on herbs and won't give any information as to usage. It seems that a number of people spout the same information in its brief entirety. There are those who have studied their herbs and those who have not. Be careful.

The herbs that are contained in this chapter would all have been found in Northern Europe, Scandinavia and the U.S. These are plants, which would have been readily available to the Vikings and their forerunners.

As this is a book about Northern Traditions, there are many herbs, which will be conspicuous in their absence. Do not be alarmed. These can be used in Norse magic, as well. The Vikings would have come across many of them in their...um...'trading missions' and incorporated their use. Norse work is very adaptable.

HOW HERBS MAY BE USED

There are many ways to use herbs magically, and some ways work better for some herbs than others. Some herbs require a very specific way in which to work. Those things will be covered within those specific herbs.

Infusion

Simply put, this is a tea: heating water and allowing the herb properties to infuse into the hot water. An infusion is normally drunk, but not always, as you will see.

145

Bath
Infuses the properties of the herb into the bathwater. This can be a very effective way to use certain herbs. Magical baths are also a good way to prepare for ritual work.

Smoke or Incense
Also a very effective way of using some herbs or effecting certain workings. The herb is simply burned and the smoke does the work.

Oils and Ointments
The herb is infused into a base, such as vegetable or olive oil, or for ointments, a base of shortening or lard. These can then be rubbed on an object or the body.

Sachets
A bag, filled with the herb that is places in a drawer, under a pillow, or hung somewhere to release the properties into the space. Similar to that is the Mojo Bag, or Medicine Bag.

THE LIST OF HERBS
Agrimony   Agrimonia Eupatoria
Synonyms: Cocklebur, Sticklewort
Part used: the herb

PROTECTION
Use in sachets and spells to banish negative energy and spirits. Agrimony is useful for protection against evil and poison. It will reverse spells sent against you by someone else.

Agrimony breaks spells and sends them back to the sender. Empower the leaves and place them in a sachet to hang above the door or carry on your person.

In spells, Agrimony can also be burned upon the altar, sending negative influence back to the hexer. A very effective way to use this method, is to burn Agrimony outside and allow the wind to carry the smoke back to the hexer.

Basil   Ocimum Basilicum
Synonym: American Dittany, Witch's Herb, Sweet Basil
Part used: the herb

CLEANSING
As protection against evil, strew it around on the floor, use in a magical bath, or make an infusion and sprinkle the furniture. So used, it protects by cleansing from unwanted energy and past use.

Basil increases sympathy between two people. Sometimes, therefore, it is used as a love herb in cooking. The reason it is successful this way is because of the sympathy it causes – the love would have to already be there. It will not cause someone to fall in love with you. It's very misunderstood because of this.

Club Moss   Lycopodium clavatum
Synonym: Foxtail, Selago, Wolf Claw
Part used: The spores only

EMPOWERMENT
Gives blessings from the gods and protection. This is a powerful plant. As the gods appreciate a strong person coming before them, any help to that effect is welcome. Use in a magical bath along with Basil before entering the realm of the gods, especially Odin.

Deerstongue Frasera Speciosa;Liatris Odoratissima
Synonym: Vanilla Leaf, Wild Vanilla
Part used: leaves

PSYCHIC ACUITY
Enhances psychic abilities when worn. This ability connects it to the Vanir. Though Deerstongue is not used to foretell the future, it can enhance your abilities to sense the world around you. This can be very handy, when one is in unfamiliar surroundings.

Carry it in a sachet.

147

Eyebright   Euphrasia Officinalis

Synonym: Euphrosyne, Red Eyebright
Part used: the herb

MENTAL ACUITY

Enhances mental and psychic abilities. It clears the mind and aids the memory. It is advised that this be used in connection with Deerstongue and Agrimony when one is on unfamiliar ground. Because of Eyebright's ability to enhance mental acuity, it is a great aid in seeing the truth of a matter.

Brew into an infusion or carry in a sachet.

Feverfew   Chrysanthemum Parthenium

Synonym: Featherfew, Febrifuge plant
Part used: the herb

PROTECTION FROM ACCIDENTS

Feverfew gets its name from its traditional use as a febrifuge: an herb used to lower body temperature. It is currently being studied as a ward against migraines, as well. In this case it is brewed as an infusion.

In the Middle Ages, Feverfew was wound around the wrist to protect from colds and fevers. Because so many accidents can be caused when one is not fully aware (due to fevers), the plant was used to ward against accidents.

Wind it around your wrist or carry it in a sachet.

Goldenrod   *Solidago*

Synonym: Common Goldenrod, Sweet Goldenrod, Blue Mountain Tea, Wound weed
Part used: the stalk and flower

DIVINATION

Goldenrod is one of the best herbs to aid in divination that I am aware of. As such, it is an herb that has been truly blessed by the Vana-gods. It is said to have the power to find hidden springs of water and hidden treasures of gold and silver.

Any of the members of the Solidago family will have these properties. It is a prevalent plant, which grows just about anywhere, from hillsides to roadsides

Goldenrod can be used in various ways. It can be infused into a tea, burned upon the altar, or it can be prayed over and cast upon the surface of a body of water.

TREES AND WOODS

There are a number of woods with specific powers, which were used by the ancient Norse and Vikings. This is by no means a complete list, but many of the more important ones have been listed. In many cases, these woods are referenced in the Edda and mythology. There are lists which attempt to connect every type of wood to a specific deity. I disagree with this practice. I do, however, call these the Nine Sacred Woods (and that's MY term for them). Many of them do have a direct connection to a Norse deity.

YEW

Yew is prized for making bows, because of its strength and flexibility. It is a wood of war and hunting. In a magical context, it is very good for Rune workings of an active protective nature. It is associated with Tew, as well as Odin, Ull and Skadhi.

OAK

Oak is known for its strength. It is much heavier than Yew and is exceptional for making shields and barriers. Brunhilde called Sigurd the "Oak of Battle," which was to say that his strength and trustworthiness could always be counted upon. This will give you an idea as to how this wood can be used magically.

BIRCH

Birch is a tree, which has direct connections to Freyja. It is also only one of two trees to have its own Rune, which will tell you how useful and important it was to Norse culture. Birch is still used today in knife handles, medicine and cosmetics. It has antimicrobial components, which cleanse. The light oil from the young buds is good for keeping gnats away.A tea from the inner bark can also induce dreams. Birch has associations to the passage of death and is very useful for protecting the soul on such a journey. Magically and medicinally, Birch can be used to ease labor pains, Sciatica and Rheumatism. Birch leaves are also used in the Sauna, leaving one with a wonderfully cleansed feeling. The essential oil has been used to treat skin eruptions.

CEDAR

A wood of protection, one only has to look at its physical attributes to see how this wood can be used magically, as well. Chests and closets are lined with Cedar to protect things. Because of its

150

protective nature, a Cedar branch is used to sprinkle the blood at the Blots.

PINE
Because of the proliferation of Pine, how quickly it grows and spreads, aging for years, it was known as a wood associated with prosperity. Pine is an Evergreen. Just as it is green in Summer and Winter, so true prosperity lasts in good times and bad. Pine can be burned on a fire as part of a spell. It also works well in making magical objects to draw prosperity. Pine also has a protective quality. The sap was extracted and boiled down to make pitch, which was used to cover walls and beams of houses. Pine is associated with Njord and Frey.

ASH
The hardest wood in Northern Europe, Ash is used for spear shafts, staffs and, like Oak, axe handles. Odin and his brothers fashioned the first man from the Ash tree. Yggdrasil, the World tree, is Ash. A very masculine wood, it is life giving, protective and strong.

ELM
Just as man was fashioned from Ash, so woman was fashioned from Elm. Its connection to Frigg is where we get the idea of the "wise old Elm". In Norse culture, it was known as a very feminine wood. This is not to say it was not strong, but rather, known more for its wisdom.

APPLE
When the ancients talked about Apple, they were referring to the Crabapple. It grows wild in Northern Europe and is the Grandmother of all the domestic varieties. It can be used in dream work to foretell of love and long life. The fruit of the Apple tree has long been considered an aid to health and a gift of Apples is a blessing, indeed. From the fragrance of the blossom to the wood and fruit, Apple is associated with life and health. Hence, it is associated with Freyja, as well as Idun.

HAZEL
Hazel is associated with judgment and protecting the sacred space. For proper thinking on a matter, cut a bind rune on a Hazel disk and keep it on your person.

Hazel poles were placed in the ground and cords strung from pole to pole to cordon off the area where judgments were to take place at the Althing. So marking it made the area sacred. Its association with judgment in matters connects it to Forseti and Baldur.

A LITTLE ABOUT METALS

Metals had certain connections and uses in the ancient culture, too. We can infer connections between certain deities and metals, but not all deities had such connections. To do so is an over generalization, or outright assumption. Though I am not going into depth about them, there are a few things to keep in mind about some metals.

IRON

Iron was used for weapons, hinges, nails and a plethora of other things, because of its strength and versatility. A most useful metal then, as now. In some cultures, it had negative connotations, when dealing with beings of the Faerie Realms. This is not so in the Norse mythology. The greatest smith is Volund, who is of Elvin race. This, in itself, connects it positively to the Elves, though he, himself, led a depressing existence.

BRASS

Up until Iron was introduced, many of the things mentioned above were made of Brass. Brass is an alloy of Tin and Copper. It is easily forged and considerably softer and lighter than Iron. And it was more easily polished. What we call the Bronze Age should be more aptly named the Brass Age. The two terms, Bronze and Brass were interchangeable and in the ancient writings meant the same thing: Brass. But what we call Bronze, today, is an alloy that includes Zinc. Zinc wasn't discovered until the mid 1800's.

SILVER

At one time, silver was more sought after than gold. It smelts easily and is very malleable. It could, therefore be used for very intricate and complex designs. Because of its softness, however, it was not used for weapons. Many old tales suggest a connection between silver and the Moon. This, being the case, would make it a very masculine metal.

GOLD

Throughout history, Gold has been one of the most sought after precious metals. Wars have been fought over it and people have died for it. It's been exchanged for everything from food to freedom. The Norse were no different than anyone else. If Silver is the metal of the Moon, then Gold is the metal of the Sun. It would,

153

then, also be feminine. When Loki cut off Sif's hair the Dwarves replaced it with pure gold.

COPPER AND TIN (ALSO SEE BRASS)

Copper has been used by man longer than any other known metal. Its use dates back around 10,000 years, but in Europe it was used for making tools around 2-3000 years ago. Its use for weapons did not become widespread until the discovery of Tin, which made if harder.

The mining of Tin was one reason why the Romans were so interested in Europe, especially the British Isles. By itself, it was used for armor plating, but when mixed with Copper to become Brass it could be made into weapons of the first order. The Brass weapons made in Europe were of a better quality than those produced in other parts of the world.

POETIC AND MUSICAL STYLES

Music has been a part of culture since man first learned he could make sounds to express himself. Along the way, a few have learned just how magical the use of music can be. It's not just a part of our mundane culture, but a part of our spiritual nature, not to mention our emotional expression and growth. We have learned to use music as a teaching tool, recite history and tell the future. But music can also be used to effect haling and change. It can be used to raise and lower energy – not just emotional, but magical. Music can be used to summon, banish and establish a sacred space. It is the most useful, all-purpose, and personal tool I know.

For music to touch the heart and the emotions, it must come FROM the heart and emotions. Many years ago, some computer wizards got together and fed the rules of music theory into a computer and programmed it to write a fugue (if you don't know what a fugue is, it's not important –only that it is a complex form of music). The fugue, though technically perfect, was boring. There was no expression of will and intent behind it. Remember, please, that a computer is just a large box of wires and stuff and it only does what it's told. I think there's a parallel, here, between music and magic. No, I'm going to stay on task.

Most mythologies refer to the gods singing for one reason or another. Usually, this was done for creative reasons. As with wine, most pantheons have at least one deity to whom music is attributed. The Norse have Odin and Braggi. The Romans have Mercurius. The Greeks attribute music to the Muses (hence the word, 'music'). The Celts have many, ranging from the Morrhigan to the gods Dagda and Belenos (and more, depending on the season and time of life). The list could go on.

Many old grimoires make reference to singing spells. Some even use the terms 'sing' and 'whisper' interchangeably. Many Pagan groups, nowadays, use a repetitive form of chant to raise and lower energy during their rites and celebrations. Words like 'chant' and 'enchantment' have the same Latin root word (cantus) meaning, song.

Music can be as simple as one note sung from the heart or as complicated as a twelve-tone melody. This is more difficult than you think. Most music in our culture is based on five tones or less.

155

Here is an important point I don't want you to miss: Music, like any other energy work, is another tool for you to use. The greatest detriment to the expression of either voice or instrument is the lack of confidence. How often were so many of us told, "You can't sing," or "Stop! That sounds terrible!" To make a corollary; for how many generations have we, as a culture been told that, "Magic is only something in fantasy books. If it ever existed, it doesn't, anymore." We do know, however, that both music and magic exist and can be used by anyone who is willing to learn and explore it. Now that I've gotten that out of the way, let's talk about Norse styles of music and poetry.

There are many styles of music and poetry that have been isolated and discovered by those who know such things. Understanding the style and symmetry in which the ancient Norse lay is written can give us clues to translation, importance of subject, and even speech patterns. It can also give us guidelines for writing new magical verse. The melodic styles may be lost to us, but the lyrical styles are not.

Fornyrdislag is commonly translated 'ancient verse.' It is a style composed in four-line stanzas, separated into half-lines, called *stafr*. The second half-line is called the *hofudstafr*, or 'main-stave.' These are separated by a rhetorical break in the flow of the line, called a *caesura*. The number of syllables per line may vary, but only two will be stressed syllables.

Is the wise ruler	here at home?
Will that ruler	speak with me?
A friendless traveler	needs to talk
Gladly would I see	Gripir soon.

From Gripispa, vs. 2

Malahattr means 'speech verse' and is very similar to *Fornyrdislag*. It, too, is generally composed in four-line stanzas separated into half-lines by a *caesura*. What makes malahattr different is that it may contain more syllables per line and allows for up to three stressed syllables.

> Would it be a good thing   Frigg, were I to go
> And make a visit to Vafthrudnir?
> I've been longing to match my lore
> Against the giant's wisdom.

156

The reason that these are so important is how they were used. Different styles were used in different ways, to promote different ideas within the listenership. And the Skalds were schooled in these styles.

Ljodahatter is another style that was used in the Eddas. It is an important and very specific one. Within the *Ljodahattr* style is another device called *Galdralog*, or, Magic verse. This device was used to emphasize a particular thought by repeating it, with a slight variation; thus, giving it weight.

> 'Tis time to chant on the sage's seat
> At the Well of Urd
> I saw, but said nothing I saw and thought
> *From Havamal vs. 111*

Or

> I frighten them with magic so that they scatter
> Heedless of hides heedless of haunts
> *From Havamal vs. 155*

The Skalds used this device to show power and importance. This makes sense, in that it was a form of magical verse. This was a style that the ancient Norse used for spell work. The power comes from its repetition of theme within the verse, taking an idea and expounding upon it in two different ways. Thus, the writer covered all bases as well as emphasized a point.

Though we know very little about scales and melodic movement, we do know metre and lyrical style of verse. It is safe to assume, however, that not all ancient melodies were dirges, modal, or in minor keys. Writing music in major scales is not a new idea in Western music. There are far too many examples from ancient times, which we still have today, and were expressed in major scales. One such source is a Christian Hymnal. Many of the older hymns were tunes that the congregation was already familiar with, but the words were changed to express new beliefs. A prime example if this practice is the United States National Anthem. Francis Scott Key may have composed new lyrics for it but the tune was an old English drinking song, which was familiar to most people.

157

The other lyrical style I'd like to mention here is *Yoik*. This is an ancient style, which comes off more like a chant than a song, having very few lyrics (or only one word), which are sung in repetition to raise power.

Yoik, unlike *Ljodahattr* or any other form of Western music is deeply rooted in the Saami Culture and it may have been more prevalent in ancient times than it is today. In other words, it may have been used by more cultures than the Saami. But the Saami have embraced it and it is such an important part of their cultural heritage that it deserves attention and preservation.

Yoik is a style of music unlike any other. It does not need to have lyrics and gets its point across without benefit of a story line. I have heard it described as a musical, three-dimensional snapshot, which has a life of its own. Not a flat picture, but alive and tangible. If you've ever experienced *Yoik*, you will understand what I am saying. *Yoik* can express emotion, states of being, landscape, smell, touch, desire.... anything that can be sensed. The scale patterns and melodies are very hard to describe in Western musical terms. *Yoik* is very shamanic in its power and its process. For examples of *Yoik*, listen to Wimme Saari, of Finland. *Yoik* may be considered chant, but I've never heard Latin Chant with this kind of power.

158

PRAYERS AND SONGS

BRUNHILDE'S PRAYER

Heil Dag, heil dags synir, heil nott ok nipt.
Oreidhum augum litidh okkr thinig ok gefidh sitjondum sigr.

Heilir Aesir, heilir Asyjur. Heil sja in fjolnyta fold. Mal ok
mannvit tveim ok laeknishendr medhan lifum.

Trans.
*Hail Day. Hail sons of Day. Hail Night and the daughters of
Night. With eyes of love, look upon us and give us the victory
we wait for.*

*Hail the Aesir – gods. Hail the Aesir – goddesses. Consider
the blessing in the fullness of the world and healing hands
our whole life.*

PRAYER TO ACTIVATE A SPOKEN RUNE SPELL

Thoer um vindr
Thoer um vefr
Thoer um setr allar saman
A thvi thingi
Er thjothir scolo
I fulla doma fara

Trans.
Those you bind
Those you weave
Those you place together
In the Thing where the many people go into the full judgment

PRAYER OVER THE SONAR-GOLT

(Freyjasgodhi):
Ber thu minnisol minum gesti
Sva hann oll muni ordh at tina
Thessar raedu a thridhja morgni
Tha er salr risr Odni till

Trans.
(Priestess of Freyja):
To my boar bring thou that he shall bear in mind

159

The Ale of memory so as to keep these words
And think of them on the third morning
When his soul rises to Odin

(Allir):
Sva hjalpi ther holler vettir
Frigg ok Freyja ok fleiri godh

Trans.
(Everybody):
So may the holy ones help thee,
Frigg and Freyja and the favoring gods

CONSECRATION OF THE HORN

Medh vatna roti Yggdrasillir
Medh handa ok hjarta
Medh eldra ok listir
Medh Mjollnir mark
Ek til helig i hornar

Trans.
By the waters of the roots of Yggrasil
By hand and heart
By fire and art
By the sign of Mjollnir
I consecrate this horn

PRAYER FOR THE SPRING PLANTING

Nu graer Jord sem adhan

Trans.
Now grows the Earth, green as before

OLD NORSE HAMMER HALLOWING

Helga Hammar i Norðri. Vera Vardmaðr of staði Þhisi
Helga Hammar i Austri. Vera Vardmaðr of staði Þhisi
Helga Hammar i Suðri. Vera Vardmaðr of staði Þhisi
Helga Hammar i Yfer. Vera Vardmaðr of heima Þhisi
Helga Hammar i Undir. Vera Vardmaðr of heima Þhisi

Þor. Haffan Þor mikil sterkt
Vera Vardmaðr of staði Þhisi Þin
Þor Þakket við. Þor heðrek við.
Þor gefak Þakkae fyr Mollnir hammer Þin.
Það er lokit

Trans.

Holy Hammer of the North. Be guardian over this, our dwelling.
Holy hammer of the East. Be guardian over this, our dwelling
Holy Hammer of the South. Be guardian over this, our dwelling
Holy Hammer of the West. Be guardian over this, our dwelling.
Holy Hammer above.   Be guardian over this our home
Holy Hammer beneath. Be guardian over this, our home.

Thor. Thor of great strength
Be guardian over this, our dwelling
Thor, we thank you. Thor, we honor you
Thor, we give thanks for your hammer, Mollnir.
It is finished

DELLING'S MORNING PRAYER
Aful Asum enn alfum frama. Hyggjo Hroptatyr!

Trans.
Strength to the Aesir and creativity to the Elves. Wisdom to Odin.

RIDHA VIT (A PRAYER FOR THE DEAD)
Ridha Vit nu skulum kvad in rika _____
Groena heima godha Odni at segja
At un mun alvaldr koma a han sjalfan at sja

Trans.
And now let us ride, says the rich _____
Across the green home of the gods and say to Odin
Lo! A great king is coming to see you.

161

GLOSSARY

Below is a list of some of the terms and abbreviations used in this book, which may be helpful to the reader. Since the book goes into detail about some terms, I have omitted those from the glossary.

AESIR
The pantheon of Norse deities who follow Odin as Supreme lord of all. Their offices generally include war, protection, wisdom, Rune magic and creativity.

ALTHING
(See Thing) A Thing held on a countrywide basis. Laws were established, fates decided and fines were levied. But it was also a time for the people to come together and trade, do business and have fun, much like the old idea of the Fair.

ASADIS
The female deities of the Aesir

ASMEGIR
Lif and Liefthraser. They are under the god's protection and live with Baldur in the Underworld. They become the new parents of mankind, after the destruction of the races at Ragnarok.

ASRP
Anglo-Saxon Rune Poem

BRAGGARKUPP
A horn, which is drunk at the feasts and blots. During the drinking, either vows are made before men and gods, or one boasts about one's accomplishments. This is where we get the term 'bragging.'

DIS
A Norse female deity. The plural is *Disir*.

GALDRWERK
A magical tradition of the Norse. It is based on songs, spells and incantaions.

GINNUNGAGAP
The expanse of primordial waters surrounding the worlds. Odin, Vili and Ve filled it with Ymir's blood to make the seas.

163

GODHI	A priest, or leader
HOFGODI	A chief priest, temple priest, or ultimate authority
HOSTAGE	In ancient times, hostages were exchanged after war to insure peace. These people were treated with all courtesy. In modern times we tend to equate the term with prisoner.
KENNING	A poetic device to name something by descriptors. Ex: 'War Weeds' for armor. Comes from the ON word Kynna (to make known)
NRP	Norwegian Rune Poem
OIRP	Old Icelandic Rune Poem
RAGNAROK	Usally translated as "The Twilight of the Gods." A closer translation would be "Storm of Powers." This is the apocalyptic battle at the end of the world, as we know it. Ragnarok will then usher in a new age for Man and the Earth.
SKALD	The singers, story-tellers and historians of the Nordic Peoples
SNORRI	Snorri Sturluson, an Icelander in the *1200's* who compiled the Prose Edda. His efforts revived an interest in preserving the old ways and many of the manuscripts.
SONARGOLT	A sacrificial goat, which was eaten at the Midsvaetrablot. The men laid hands on it and placed the greatness of their accomplishments within. The Braggarkupp accompanied the Rite of the Sonargolt.
THING	A representative body, much like city fathers, or elders. They met to decide in civil cases and establish local regulations.
TOOTH FEE	The gift given a child when his/her first tooth

164

comes in. This sign was generally understood to mean that the child would live, as infant mortality was very high in ancient times

VANADIS	The female deities of the Van or Vanic pantheon
VANIR	An older pantheon of Norse deities, which is more Earth-based than the Aesir. Their offices generally include prosperity, fertility, foresight, and the oversight of the workings of the Earth and Seidh magic.
WEREGILD	The price paid for a death. This was paid by the killer, or family of the killer, to the family of the deceased and was done as an act of evening the score. When weregild was paid and accepted, no vengeance could be taken for the death..
WIGHT/VATTR	A catchall term, simply meaning any being of human-like appearance. This also includes supernatural beings. The word normally carries an undertone of misfortune
WIGHT/VATTR	A catchall term, simply meaning any being of human-like appearance. This also includes supernatural beings. The word normally carries an undertone of misfortune
WYRD	Commonly defined as 'Fate', it can also refer to the lines of connection we have with others.

PRONUNCIATION GUIDE

Below is a short guide to help you in pronouncing Old Norse words and names. A number of the sounds are similar, however, there are a few which are sounded differently than what conventional writing allows for. This is not a complete guide, but it's enough to correct a number of common mistakes.

LETTER	Sound	English Example(s)	Old Norse Example(s)
a	short a	land, father	Mann, Har
e	short e	met	Hel
i	ee	fiend	Litr
o	long o	tone	floti
	short o	tong	hof
u	oo	crude	luka
y	oo	*(none)*	fylgja
ae	long a	*(none)*	Midsvaetr
au	ah-oo	round	baugr
ei	eh-ee	*(none)*	beita
ey	eh-oo	feud	dreyri
oe	o-ee	going, coin	loekr

Double Consonants are held out longer than single consonants *(ex. bok (book) and bokki (fellow)*

h in front of n, l, v and r is silent *(ex. hrekja (to drive away)*

R plays many roles. At the beginning of a word or following a vowel, it was rolled. However, following a consonant at the end of a word, it was silent. The interesting thing about this letter is that it had the value more related to *zh* than what we would consider an r sound. In this way it has more likely evolved into ß, or the double S we find in German. As the language developed into East and West Norse, a vowel (generally an 'i') was placed before the r, which would then be rolled.

167

ADDITIONAL NOTES

HOD

It has always intrigued me that such a great warrior as Hod was blind. In point of fact, he was never known as a blind god to our ancient ancestors. Only Snorri called him blind and it's stuck, ever since.

In the late 900's, Olaf Hoskuldsson built a large, new house and mead hall at his farm, Hjardaholt, in Iceland (*Laxdaelasaga 29*). He had an artist come in and paint scenes from the Edda and many stories of the gods on the walls, ceiling and crossbeams. Olaf, had a Grand Opening and a well-known skald, Ulf Uggason, was there. Ulf, composed a poem about Olaf and the scenes on the walls, one of which was the death of Baldur. This poem is called 'Husdrapa' (which means, "Song for the House") But, Husdrapa is not talking about the Eddic tales. It's talking about the artwork in Olaf's house. The only way that the artist could depict Hod's delusion by Loki was to paint him as a blind god.

Snorri had access to Husdrapa and used it in his research for the Prose Edda. Only fragments of Husdrapa now exist today, however, we know that Skaldskaparmal drew heavily from Husdrapa and that Snorri also referred to it in Gylfaginning, as well.

LEIKN

The term that is used in the mythology is ljotvaxinn -'ugly-grown.' This is a horse, which is born with three legs. The birth of a three-legged horse carries the superstition of bringing sickness and plague.

THE ASMEGIR

I must say that I like Hollander's translation of the name Hleifthrasa; 'Longing for Life.' It's much more poetic and in keeping with the feel of the future of the Asmegir.

CALENDARS AND BLÓTS AND CELEBRATIONS

I mentioned that the ancient Norse calendars were not Lunar. There is evidence, however, that since the calendar that was standardized by Iceland, the times and dates for Blóts and

169

Celebrations were taken from a starting point, being the first full moon after the Vinternal. I would encourage the reader to study the Primstav and Runic Calendars from the 1000's and forward. Though they were heavily influenced by the Church, there are marked events, which, by that time, had become more cultural, but were, in fact, ancient Norse rites and celebrations.

Much has been made about the Thorrablót, not included in this calendar. There is a reason. First, the Thorrablót is a local celebration originaly held in the Orkneys to honor ancient King Thorri, who, by that tradition, is actually Thor, the deity (*see Orkneyingasaga*) By this mythology, he is also the father of Goi, mentioned in the section on Calendars. The second reason us that the Thorrablót was held at the Midsvaetr. There is no reason not to honor Thor with a Blót, but, since it is dedicated to Frey and Njord, I would suggest finding another time of year to do it.

ODINIRVEIDHIFOR
The word literally means 'Odin's Wild Hunt.' In ancient times, it was well known that the hunt took place in the deepest of winter. Many people celebrate it during the time of the Midsvaetr. However, according to the Anglo-Saxon Chronicles, it was actually witnessed by many in England on the night of February 6th, 1127. This is as good a date as any, and we have an actual date at which to celebrate it. InSouthern Sweden, it was common for people to carry a bit of steel and a bit of bread in one's pocket. That way, if they encountered Odin, they could drop the steel in front of him and he would not harm them. The bread was for the same reason, in case they encountered Odin's dogs.

THREE CUPS
The three cups represent the three fountains, which feed the roots of Yggdrasil: Hvergelmir, in the north, feeds the northern-most root with icy salt water. The central root is fed by Mimir's well, which is also called Son. The southern root is fed by Urd's Well, also known as the Strength of the Earth (Jardr Magn or, Urdr Magn – Urd's Strength).

RADH
In the mythology of the Nordic folk, particularly in Sweden, there is a classification of beings called the Ra. They were lake wights (Sjora), woodland wights (Skogsra) and mountain wights (Bergra). If a man was alone in any of the areas inhabited by them, he might

170

encounter them…sexually. The Ra, then tended to show their gratitude by protecting the man from things like fire, flood and sickness. It is my belief that this promise of protection is what gave rise to the placing of ᚱ above the door of the house. The term, 'at rada,' means to govern or rule over. But, it also means 'to have one's way with.'

HYMISKVIDHA

I must say something here about Hymiskvidha; an Eddic tale, which is somewhat disregarded by many experts. Some scholars believe it is a tale of late origin (11th-12th Century Iceland). Others date it earlier, possibly late 10th century. My belief, however, is that there may be more, here, than meets the eye.

No skald in his right mind could have gotten away with certain things, had they not already been in the collective consciousness of the people he was singing to. How else do we reconcile equating Veur with Thor? More to the point, how do we account for Tyr being called "good-hearted?"

This is my opinion: the skald was German, not of Icelandic or Scandinavian origin. The word, 'veur' (veor) is Old Dutch (5th to 12th century) surviving from Proto-Germanic. Veur was an area in what is now the Netherlands. We do know that many places (settlements, rivers, mountains, etc) were named for deities. Examples include Minervois France (Minerva), London England (Lugh), Skedvi Sweden (Skadhi), the Boyne River in Ireland (Boann), Mount Olympus in Greece, and more. This unnamed skald reconciled his own understanding of the gods with his audience's understanding. Is Veur a mainland European god, who's attributes resemble Thor's? Quite possibly, on a local level. It would be interesting to locate ancient skaldic tales that equate Veur with Donnar. That might give us a clue. Another possibility is that, though the skald sang of Tyr and Veur, whoever recorded it in Iceland changed the name of Veur to Thor. In only one passage (*vs 11*) was he not able to do that.

Hymiskvidha also alludes to Thor's lineage as being Vanic in vs 3. Why would Aegir want to take vengeance on the Vanir, if Thor were not Vanic? Why not vow vengeance on the Aesir? This lends support to his relationship to Frigg. Since he is also called the son of Odin, we can assume that either he was adopted by Odin or that the lineage was understood as coming though the maternal line,

171

not, necessarily, though a paternal lineage. It is the same reason that Frey can be called 'best of the Aesir' (*Skirnismal 3 and Lokasenna 37*).

Now, we come to the question of Tyr. In the south, Tyr was worshipped as the god above all..even Wodan. The Tyr that is talked about in Hymiskvidha is not the Tyr that was worshipped in Scandinavia. This is an older, more ancient deity that is descended directly from the Jotn. Hymisvidha clearly states this in verses 8 and 9, where it mentions his grandmother (*vs 8*) and calls him a direct descendant (*vs 9*). This Tyr is a god of justice, as well, which is part of the complication. In the northern traditions, he is the son of Odin, the god of justice and protector of warriors, whose cause is just. Earlier in the book, I mentioned that in the south, Tyr was not known as having lost a hand to Fenrir. This is why: he is not the same deity.

BIBLIOGRAPHY

Cunningham, Scott, *Encyclopedia of Magical Herbs*
St Paul: Llewellyn Publications 1994

du Chaillu, Paul, *The Viking Age* New York: Scribner's Books
1889

Flowers, Stephen, Chisholm, James, ed. *A Source Book of Seid*
Smithville: Runa-Raven Press 2002

Gordon, E.V., *An Introduction to Old Norse*
New York: Oxford University Press 1927

Guerber, H.A., The Mythology of the Norsemen
New York: Dover Press 1992

Gundarsson, K.H., *Our Troth The Ring of Troth* 1993

H.R. Ellis Davidson*, Gods and Myths of Northern Europe*
London: Penguin Books 1988

Hollander, Lee, *The Poetic Edda* Austin: University of Texas Press
1962

Howard, Michael, *Understanding Runes* San Francisco: Thorsons
1995

Hveberg, Harald, *Of Gods and Giants* Oslo: Tanum-Norli 1976

Jones, Prudence, Pennick, Nigel, *A History of Pagan Europe*
Barnes and Noble 1995

Magnusson, Magnus, *Lindisfarne* London: Oriel Press 1984

Magnusson, Magnus, *Vikings!* New York: EP Dutton 1980

Newcomer and Andrews ed *Twelve Centuries of English Poetry
and Prose* Chicago: Scott Foreman and Co. 1910

Rydberg, Victor, *Our Fathers' Godsaga*
New York: iUniverse, Inc reprint 2003

Rydberg, Viktor, *Investigations into Germanic Mythology Vol.II*
New York: iUniverse Inc 2004

Rydberg, Viktor, *Researches in Teutonic Mythology*
Honolulu: University Press of the Pacific 2004

Smiley, Jane, ed. *Sagas of the Icelanders*
New York: Liefur Eiriksson Publishing 1997

Terry, Patricia, *Poems of the Vikings*
New York: Bobbs-Merrill Co, Inc 1969

Thistleton-Dyer, T.F., The Folklore of Plants
Detroit: Singing Tree Press 1968

Thorson, Edred, *Witchdom of the* True Smithville: Runa-Raven
Press 1999

Wagner, Dr W. *Asgard and the Gods*
New York: EP Dutton and Co. 1917

Blecher, Lone T. and George, *Swedish Folktales and Legends*
New York: Pantheon Books 1993

Taylor P.B. and Auden W.H. *The Elder Edda (First Edition)* New
York: Vintage Books 1970

Sturluson, *Snorri The Younger Edda* (Transl. Rasmus B.
Anderson) Chicago: Scott Foresman and Co 1901

Tacitus, *The Agricola and Germania* (transl K.B. Townshend)
London: Methuen & co 1894

Heide, Eldar (2004) *Spinning Seidh: Old Norse Religion in Long-
term Perspectives, Origins, Changes and Interactions*, Lund
Sweden June 3-7, 2004
        Nordic Academic Press

Bellows, H.A. (Transl) *The Poetic Edda American Scandinavian
Foundation*: New York 1923

174

RECOMMENDED READINGS

These books are a good place to start your research into customs and practices of ancient East Norse ways.

Hollander, Lee, *The Poetic Edda* Austin: University of Texas Press 1962

Jones, Prudence, Pennick, Nigel, *A History of Pagan Europe*. Barnes and Noble 1995

Rydberg, Victor, *Our Fathers' Godsaga* New York: iUniverse, Inc reprint 2003

Terry, Patricia, *Poems of the Vikings* New York: Bobbs-Merrill Co, Inc 1969

Thorson, Edred, *Witchdom of the True* Smithville: Runa-Raven Press 1999

ALSO RECOMMENDED

Any translations of:

Anglo-Saxon Rune Poem

Old Icelandic Rune Poem

Norwegian Rune Poem

Made in the USA
Lexington, KY
01 June 2018